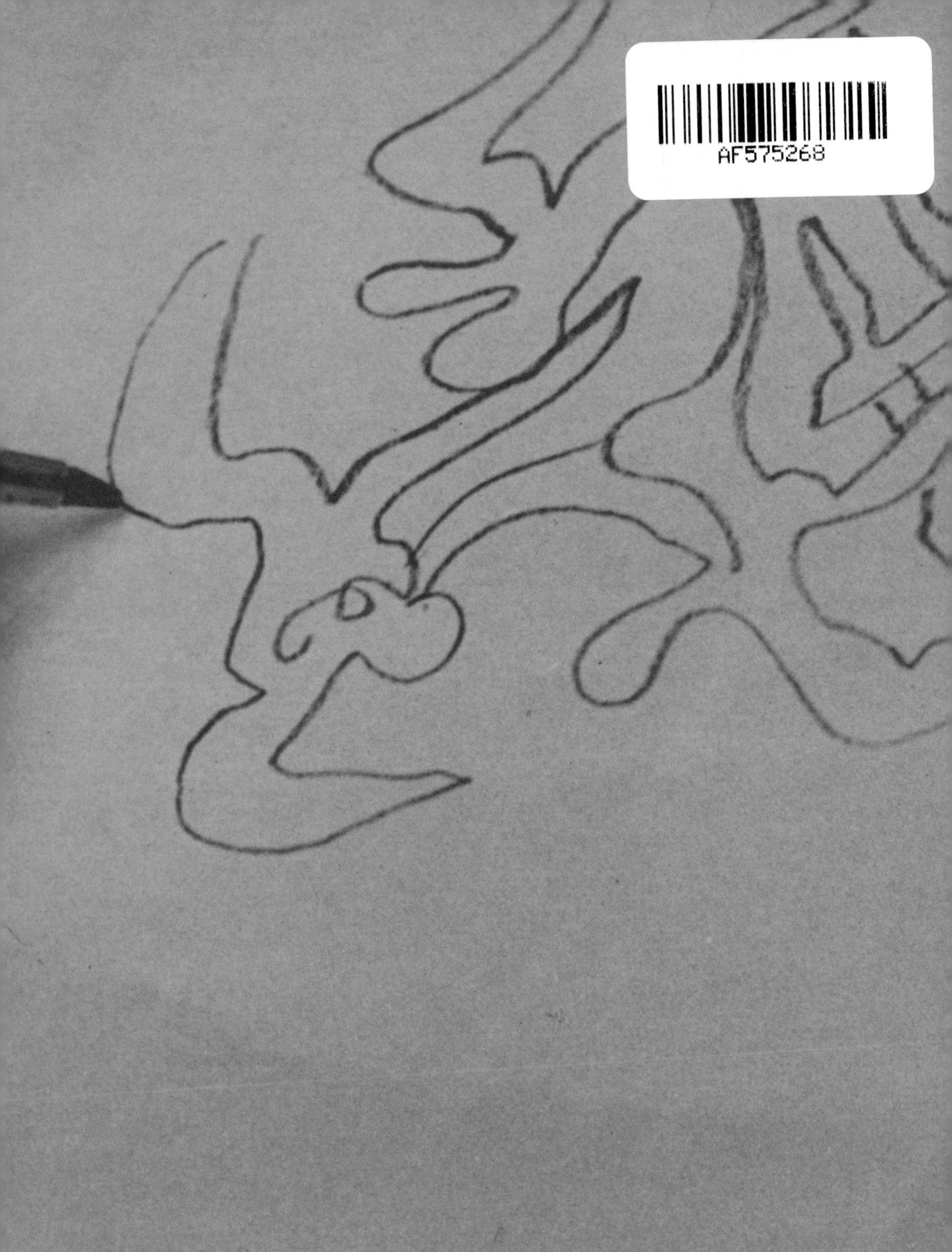

MATISSE AS PRINTMAKER

WORKS FROM THE PIERRE AND TANA MATISSE FOUNDATION

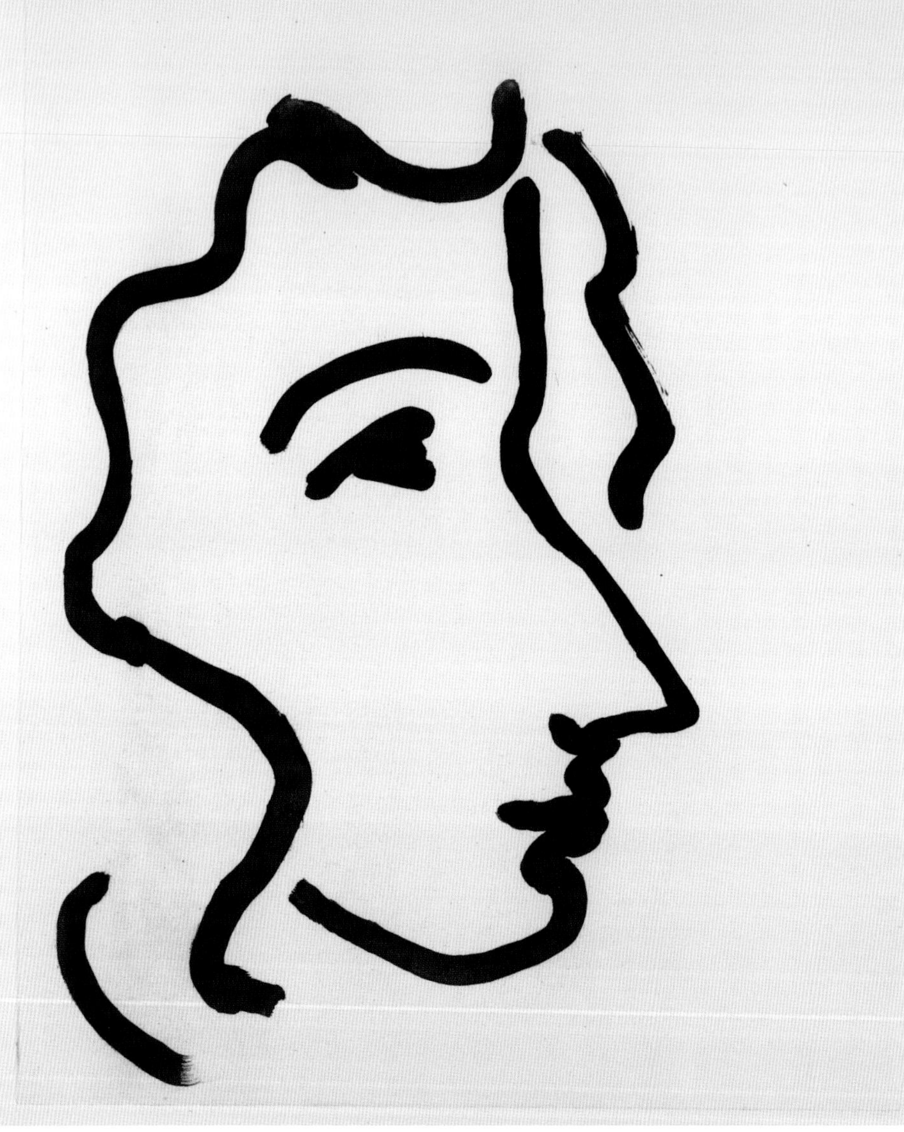

MATISSE AS PRINTMAKER

WORKS FROM THE PIERRE AND TANA MATISSE FOUNDATION

Jay McKean Fisher

with an essay by
William S. Lieberman

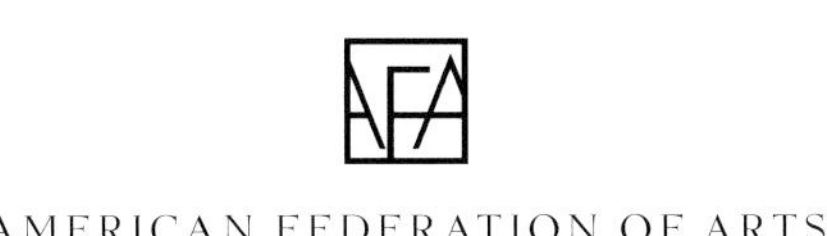

AMERICAN FEDERATION OF ARTS

This catalogue is published in conjunction with *Matisse as Printmaker: Works from the Pierre and Tana Matisse Foundation*, an exhibition organized by the American Federation of Arts and the Pierre and Tana Matisse Foundation.

The American Federation of Arts is a nonprofit institution that organizes art exhibitions for presentation in museums around the world, publishes exhibition catalogues, and develops education programs.

Guest Curator: Jay McKean Fisher
Publications Manager: Michaelyn Mitchell
Managing Curator: Suzanne Ramljak
Designers: Luke Hayman and Shigeto Akiyama, Pentagram
Editor: David Frankel
Indexer: Susan Burke

Front cover: Matisse signature from *Henri Matisse* (Paris: Galeries Georges Petit, 1931).
Back cover: *Crouching Nude I* (cat. no. 52)
Frontispiece: *Nadia in Sharp Profile* (cat. no. 58)
End paper: Matisse drawing an illustration (unpublished) for *Florilège des amours de Ronsard* on a lithographic stone, 1948. Detail of a photograph by Ina Bandy. Archives Matisse, Paris

Essay by William S. Lieberman reprinted, with permission, from *Matisse: 50 Years of His Graphic Art* (New York: George Braziller, 1956).

Published in 2009 by the American Federation of Arts.

10 9 8 7 6 5 4 3 2 1

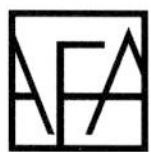

American Federation of Arts
305 East 47th Street, 10th Floor
New York, NY 10017
www.afaweb.org

Library of Congress
Cataloging-in-Publication Data

Fisher, Jay McKean, 1949–
Matisse as printmaker : works from the Pierre and Tana Matisse Foundation / by Jay McKean Fisher ; with an essay by William S. Lieberman. — 1st ed.
p. cm.
Catalog of an exhibition held at the Baltimore Museum of Art, Baltimore, Md., and three other institutions between Oct. 23, 2009 and Jan. 30, 2011.
Includes bibliographical references and index.
ISBN 978-1-885444-38-7
1. Matisse, Henri, 1869–1954—Exhibitions. I. Matisse, Henri, 1869–1954. II. Lieberman, William S. (William Slattery), 1924–2005. III. Baltimore Museum of Art. IV. Title.

NE650.M38A4 2009
769.92—dc22
2008046807

Exhibition Itinerary

The Baltimore Museum of Art
Baltimore, Maryland
October 23, 2009–January 3, 2010

Tampa Museum of Art
Tampa, Florida
February 3–April 18, 2010

The Blanton Museum of Art
University of Texas at Austin
May 23–July 25, 2010

Art Gallery of Alberta
Edmonton, Alberta, Canada
October 29, 2010–February 13, 2011

Printed in China

CONTENTS

ACKNOWLEDGMENTS

Printmaking is one of the many art forms in which Henri Matisse distinguished himself. The vibrant body of graphic works he completed during his lifetime includes more than eight hundred intaglios, lithographs, woodcuts, linoleum cuts, and monotypes. Selected from the foundation established by Matisse's son, the legendary art dealer Pierre Matisse, and his wife, Maria Gaetana (Tana), *Matisse as Printmaker: Works from the Pierre and Tana Matisse Foundation* includes examples of every type of printmaking utilized by Matisse. These works make a strong case for the significance of the series in Matisse's art and eloquently underscore the extraordinary sense of intimacy expressed in so much of his printmaking. This is in part because of the scale of the works but also due to the artist's working process and choice of subject—nudes in the studio, friends and family members, women watching fish in a bowl, leg studies, and odalisques. It has been a privilege to be able to borrow these works, all once owned by Pierre Matisse, from the Pierre and Tana Matisse Foundation and to partner with them in organizing this wonderful project.

We are very grateful to the Matisse Foundation's board members, as well as its Executive Director, Alessandra Carnielli. We also wish to warmly acknowledge the contribution of our Guest Curator, Jay McKean Fisher, Deputy Director for Curatorial Affairs and Senior Curator of Prints, Drawings, and Photographs at The Baltimore Museum of Art.

The staff of the AFA deserves recognition for their wonderful work on behalf of the exhibition and publication. I wish to first recognize Suzanne Ramljak, Curator of Exhibitions, for her contribution to the organization of this project. Michaelyn Mitchell, Director of Publications and Communications, coordinated all aspects of the production of this handsome and important catalogue, with the assistance of Amy Mazzariello, Publications/Communications Assistant. Anna Hayes, Manager of Exhibitions Administration, provided critical oversight, and Jennifer Hefner, Registrar, was responsible for preparing and touring the exhibition. I also want to acknowledge Suzanne Burke, Director of Education; Cheryl Aldridge, Director of Development; and former staff members Luis Croquer, Kathleen Flynn, Yvette Lee, and Sirena Maxfield, as well as former Director Julia Brown, under whose aegis the exhibition was developed.

We would like to acknowledge the superb work of Luke Hayman and Shigeto Akiyama of Pentagram in designing this catalogue, the astute editing that was done by David Frankel, and the fine work of Christopher Burke who photographed the works in the exhibition.

Finally, we recognize the museums participating in the tour of this beautiful exhibition—the Baltimore Museum of Art; the Tampa Museum of Art; the Blanton Museum of Art, University of Texas at Austin; and the Art Gallery of Alberta. It has been a great pleasure to work with them, and we thank them for being such professional and enthusiastic partners.

PAULINE WILLIS
Acting Director
American Federation of Arts

The Pierre and Tana Matisse Foundation was founded in 1995 by Maria Gaetana (Tana) Matisse to further the interests of her late husband, the great dealer of modern art, Pierre Matisse. The foundation has generously made the collection of Pierre and Tana Matisse available to museums as loans and through gifts and has also encouraged the organization of exhibitions based on its collections, such as this exhibition. I am very grateful to the foundation's board members and Executive Director Alessandra Carnielli. Without their dedication and support this exhibition would not have been possible. It was Pierre Matisse's longtime friend, William S. Lieberman, then Curator of Modern and Contemporary Art at the Metropolitan Museum of Art and a longtime trustee of the American Federation of Arts, who first suggested the idea of working with the AFA to organize an exhibition from the foundation's Matisse print holdings. Today's scholars remain grateful to Bill Lieberman for his early curatorial research and perceptive writing on Matisse's prints and illustrated books.

With the foundation's selection of the AFA to organize the exhibition, the project benefited from the talents of the AFA's former Director, Julia Brown, and Suzanne Ramljak, Curator of Exhibitions, as well as past AFA staff members involved in the early stages of the project: Kathleen Flynn, Judy Kim, Yvette Lee, and Eric Neil. Michaelyn Mitchell, Director of Publications and Communications, saw the publication through its completion with the assistance of editor David Frankel and designers Luke Hayman and Shigeto Akiyama. I have greatly benefited from the assistance of my colleagues at The Baltimore Museum of Art: Director Doreen Bolger, who encouraged my participation and the participation of the Baltimore Museum as the opening venue; Steven Mann, Director of Exhibitions, who coordinated the Baltimore venue of the exhibition; Brianna Begidian, Manager of Rights and Reproductions, who coordinated the museum's contribution of numerous reproductions for the catalogue; and Thomas Primeau, Director of Conservation and Paper Conservator, who provided valuable expertise in the discussion of print medium questions. At the museum, I am also grateful to Michelle Boardman, Rena Hoisington, Rob Morgan, Bililynn Savage, and Ann Shafer.

I also want to acknowledge Georges Matisse at the Archives Matisse (recently moved from Paris to the artist's former house and studio in Issy-les-Moulineaux), for his assistance in obtaining reproductions for the illustrations in this publication. Wanda De Guébriant at the Archives Matisse also provided valuable help. Finally, my research has been assisted by a number of colleagues, including Riva Castleman and Jack Flam; Stephanie D'Alessandro, Mark Pascale, and Kate Tierney Powell at the Art Institute of Chicago; and Sara Cooper, Mara Sprafkin, and Deborah Wye at the Museum of Modern Art.

Jay McKean Fisher

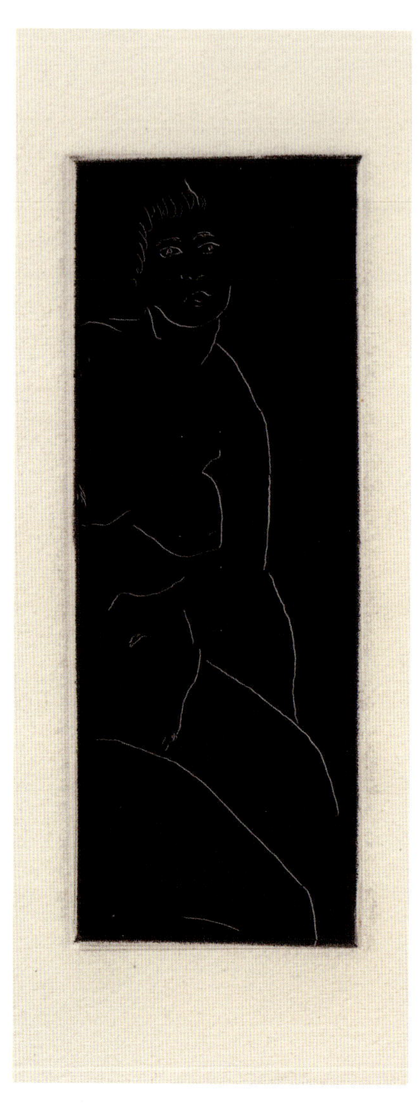

Cropped Nude II, 1914 (cat. no. 14)

INTRODUCTION

Jay McKean Fisher

Recognized foremost as a painter and colorist, Henri Matisse was also deeply engaged with making art through other mediums, such as printmaking, drawing, and sculpture, where he worked fundamentally without color. He would often move an idea from one medium to another, from drawing to sculpture, say, and then to painting or printmaking, advancing it in one medium while leaving it aside for a period in the other, only later to take it up anew. He often moved from two dimensions to three, from painting to sculpture or the reverse. All the means he adopted to advance his art were integrated by the nature of his vision, but each was understood in terms of its unique properties, its inherent challenges, and its potential for unique forms of vision. Observing Matisse's art, the viewer inevitably becomes conscious of the medium and of the way the artist worked with it to a point of resolution. This creative process remains legible, involving the viewer first in the act of observation and then in the path of revision to the point of transformation. Matisse's intense and prolific involvement with printmaking must be recognized as an equivalent means of creative expression, one that offers the viewer the potential for its own kind of engagement with aspects that are central to all of Matisse's art.

At the end of Matisse's life, no museum was more dedicated to his work than the Museum of Modern Art in New York. MoMA had organized its first Matisse exhibition in 1931, and by 1934, twelve prints had entered the collection, the gift of the Baltimore collector Saidie A. May.[1] The collection continued to grow with important paintings and sculpture, and in 1951, MoMA's founding director, Alfred H. Barr, Jr., organized his great retrospective exhibition of the artist's work. It was appropriate that an American museum (the Philadelphia Museum of Art, too, had organized an earlier retrospective in 1948) gave such priority to Matisse: throughout his career, American collectors had been his most important patrons, acquiring the largest collections of his work in all media.[2] The lasting impact of Barr's exhibition results from its remarkable catalogue, which remains an essential resource for Matisse studies today.[3] In his acknowledgments, Barr writes of his debt to members of the Matisse family, particularly the artist's son Pierre but also his wife, Amélie, and his daughter, Marguerite Duthuit. William S. Lieberman, then the museum's curator of prints, played a significant role in Barr's study, undertaking (with the art historian John Rewald) crucial interviews with close associates of Matisse, most importantly Duthuit, who knew a great deal about the artist's history and studio practices.[4] She had managed his creative production, bringing order and keeping records, and at the time of the MoMA exhibition, she was at work on a catalogue of his paintings, never completed. She would eventually compile the catalogue raisonné of Matisse's prints and illustrated books, completed by her son, Claude Duthuit, in 1983.[5] Lieberman may have had much to do with Barr's inclusion of prints and illustrated books at key places in his text and of course in the exhibition; Barr acknowledged in his preface that the illustrated books, along with the sculpture, were less well-known parts of Matisse's work. Matisse's prints, too, despite their integral role in his art, still play little if any part in most retrospective exhibitions.

In the same year as the MoMA exhibition of 1951, Lieberman wrote an essay, "Illustrations by Henri Matisse," in the *Magazine of Art.* In 1955, he produced for MoMA a catalogue on the artist's etchings; and in 1956, he published a book on the prints, *Matisse: 50 Years of His Graphic Art.*[6] These were the first comprehensive writings on Matisse's printmaking that were widely available. In particular, Lieberman's essay from the last of these books, which is reprinted in the present publication, not only established a sensible chronology for Matisse's prints but also in its focus on medium—etching, lithography, and linoleum cut—highlighted the link between the stylistic character of the prints in certain years and the inherent character of a chosen printmaking medium. His focus on prints assumed the integration of printmaking in the whole of Matisse's art.

Near the time of Matisse's death, in 1954, a MoMA curator was uniquely well equipped to incorporate the printed work into the overall oeuvre, since MoMA already held a substantial survey of the artist's prints in the context of a collection of modern printmaking, not to mention its growing holdings of Matisse's paintings and sculpture. By the time Lieberman wrote his catalogue on Matisse's etchings, MoMA owned more than one hundred such works. Lieberman was responsible for the acquisition of almost all of the Matisse graphics and illustrated books in MoMA's collection. In New York, the Metropolitan Museum of Art also had important Matisse print holdings, and other prints would have been available from dealers and collectors. With the donation of the Cone Collection in 1950, The Baltimore Museum of Art had the largest Matisse print collection (which Lieberman came to Baltimore to study), followed by important holdings at the Art Institute of Chicago and the Philadelphia Museum of Art. While the student of Matisse today has an overwhelming list of references to consult, in 1953 the fullness of the artist's oeuvre was just becoming known. The optimal reference for the scholar seeking a comprehensive study of an artist's work, or a focus on a medium such as printmaking, is the catalogue raisonné, but such a book was not available for Matisse until 1983, with the publication of Duthuit's catalogue of 829 prints. (A second catalogue of book projects would follow in 1988.)[7] The first truly comprehensive exhibition of Matisse's prints, with a well-illustrated catalogue, was organized in 1982, in Fribourg, by Margrit Hahnloser-Ingold, who followed up with her 1988 book *Matisse: The Graphic Work.*[8] Lieberman did have access to an important manuscript listing of Matisse prints by Carl O. Schniewind, then curator of prints and drawings at the Art Institute of Chicago. Marguerite Duthuit may also have shared with him her notes on the prints.[9]

How organized Matisse's estate was in making his prints available for viewing at this time is unclear. Access to prints available for sale was possible in New York through various galleries, including Pierre Matisse's gallery, the Weyhe Gallery, and in Paris through the great print dealer Henri Petiet (well known for his purchase of the vast stock of prints held by Ambroise Vollard), who was well connected both with

American dealers and with potential collectors in France. We also know that the art critic Walter Pach, who was close to Matisse, was selling prints in New York.[10] Fresh from the experience of the MoMA retrospective exhibition, Lieberman sought to define the artist's printmaking oeuvre and to describe the nature of Matisse's printmaking—the basics such as edition size, media, and, most important, chronology. A significant part of Lieberman's essay focuses on book illustrations, and while this aspect of Matisse's printmaking is for practical reasons beyond the scope of the present exhibition, Lieberman clearly integrates Matisse's book projects with his printmaking, especially in the later phase of his career.

Around 1950, Matisse gave each of his children—Marguerite, Jean, and Pierre—a "complete" collection of his print oeuvre with multiple impressions of most of the images. Because of the rarity of some prints and the category of one-of-a-kind monotypes, each collection was unique.[11] Subsequently, in 1981, a large part of Jean Matisse's portion was given to the Bibliothèque Nationale, Paris, and this body of work remains the largest and most comprehensive public collection of Matisse's prints. In 1935, the British National Art Collections Fund purchased ninety-one lithographs from Marguerite Duthuit. These were presented to the Victoria and Albert Museum, where they were exhibited in 1936 and, more recently, in 1972, accompanied by a catalogue by Susan Lambert with a major text on Matisse's printmaking correlating with painting and sculpture, in addition to information about the techniques used in Matisse's lithographs.[12]

The present exhibition is drawn from the collection of the artist's son, now part of the Pierre and Tana Matisse Foundation, New York. Since its founding in 1995, the foundation has been a generous supporter of Matisse studies, particularly by making its collection available to museums for important exhibitions. This is the first exhibition initiated by the foundation and is drawn entirely from its holdings. For the organization and circulation of the exhibition, the foundation selected the American Federation of Arts in New York.

Matisse's production of more than eight hundred printed images apart from those in his illustrated books sustained the ravenous appetite of American collectors and museums for Matisse during his lifetime and since. Until recent decades, his prints remained a relatively inexpensive way for collectors to own art by a great modern artist, and many were collected during his lifetime. Etta Cone, who would donate her and her sister Claribel's collection to The Baltimore Museum of Art, collected more than three hundred Matisse prints, acquiring some perhaps as early as 1906 and most from the 1920s onward. Simultaneous with the organization of this exhibition, the Pierre and Tana Matisse Foundation will make a major gift of prints to The Baltimore Museum of Art, bringing its representation of Matisse's prints to more than four hundred images, plus all but one of the artist's illustrated books. In its comprehensiveness and size, this assemblage is the most important collection of Matisse's prints in North America.

Notes to the Text

1 See John Elderfield, *Henri Matisse: Masterworks from The Museum of Modern Art* (New York: The Museum of Modern Art, 1996), p. 8.

2 See John O'Brian, *Ruthless Hedonism: The American Reception of Matisse* (Chicago: at the University Press, 1999).

3 Alfred H. Barr, Jr., *Matisse, His Art and His Public* (New York: The Museum of Modern Art, 1951).

4 Jack Flam, in a personal conversation with the author in August 2008. A review of the Barr/Lieberman correspondence between Alfred Barr and William Lieberman in the MoMA Archives, specifically letters of December 12 and 30, 1949, testifies to Lieberman's important role. Included are lists of questions from Barr and memorandum responses and correspondence from Lieberman in return. A written communication of October 2008 from Wanda De Guébriant at the Archives Matisse in Issy-les-Moulineaux, France, emphasizes Lieberman's good contacts with members of the Matisse family, especially Pierre Matisse.

5 Marguerite Duthuit and Claude Duthuit, *Henri Matisse. Catalogue raisonné de l'oeuvre gravé, 2 vols.* (Paris: Imprimerie Union, 1983).

6 William S. Lieberman, "Illustrations by Henri Matisse," *Magazine of Art*, no. 44 (December 1951): 308–14; Lieberman, *Etchings by Matisse* (New York: The Museum of Modern Art, 1955); Lieberman, *Matisse: 50 Years of His Graphic Art* (New York: George Braziller, 1956).

7 Claude Duthuit, *Henri Matisse. Catalogue raisonné des ouvrages illustrés* (Paris: Imprimerie Union, 1988).

8 Margrit Hahnloser-Ingold, *Henri Matisse. Gravures et lithographies* (Fribourg: Musée d'art et d'histoire, 1982); Hahnloser-Ingold, *Matisse: The Graphic Work* (New York: Rizzoli, 1988).

9 Lieberman, *Matisse: 50 Years of His Graphic Art,* note 1, p. 19. Carl O. Schniewind's manuscript is in the archives of the Art Institute of Chicago. According to records in the Barr papers in the MoMA archives, Schniewind was hired by Barr to catalogue the MoMA print collection (then about 1,650 objects) and completed this work between 1946 and 1949. The Art Institute has an important Matisse print collection, many prints having been acquired during Schniewind's tenure.

10 I am grateful to Stephanie D'Alessandro, the Gary C. and Frances Comer Curator of Modern Art at the Art Institute of Chicago, for this information.

11 Wanda De Guébriant of the Archives Matisse, Issy-les-Moulineaux, France, in a written communication to the author in October 2008. According to De Guébriant, Marguerite's share may have been sold to the Baroness d'Erlanger and eventually sold to MoMA in 1951, but the MoMA collection is not "complete." Research on the provenance of prints at MoMA confirms the provenance of d'Erlanger for the group of etchings that were catalogued by Lieberman in 1955, but the Duthuit connection is not noted. According to Riva Castleman, in an October 2008 communication with the author, the Weyhe Gallery was a source for many of the early MoMA print acquisitions, and research in the Lieberman papers at MoMA also contains reference to print purchases from the Galerie Chalette and the Deitsch Gallery in New York. Pierre Matisse's collection of his father's print oeuvre probably remained in France until the Pierre and Tana Matisse Foundation was established in New York. In a conversation with the author in February 2009, Claude Duthuit stated that Matisse's grandchildren also received collections of the artist's prints.

12 Susan Lambert, *Matisse Lithographs* (London: Victoria and Albert Museum, 1972), p. 5.

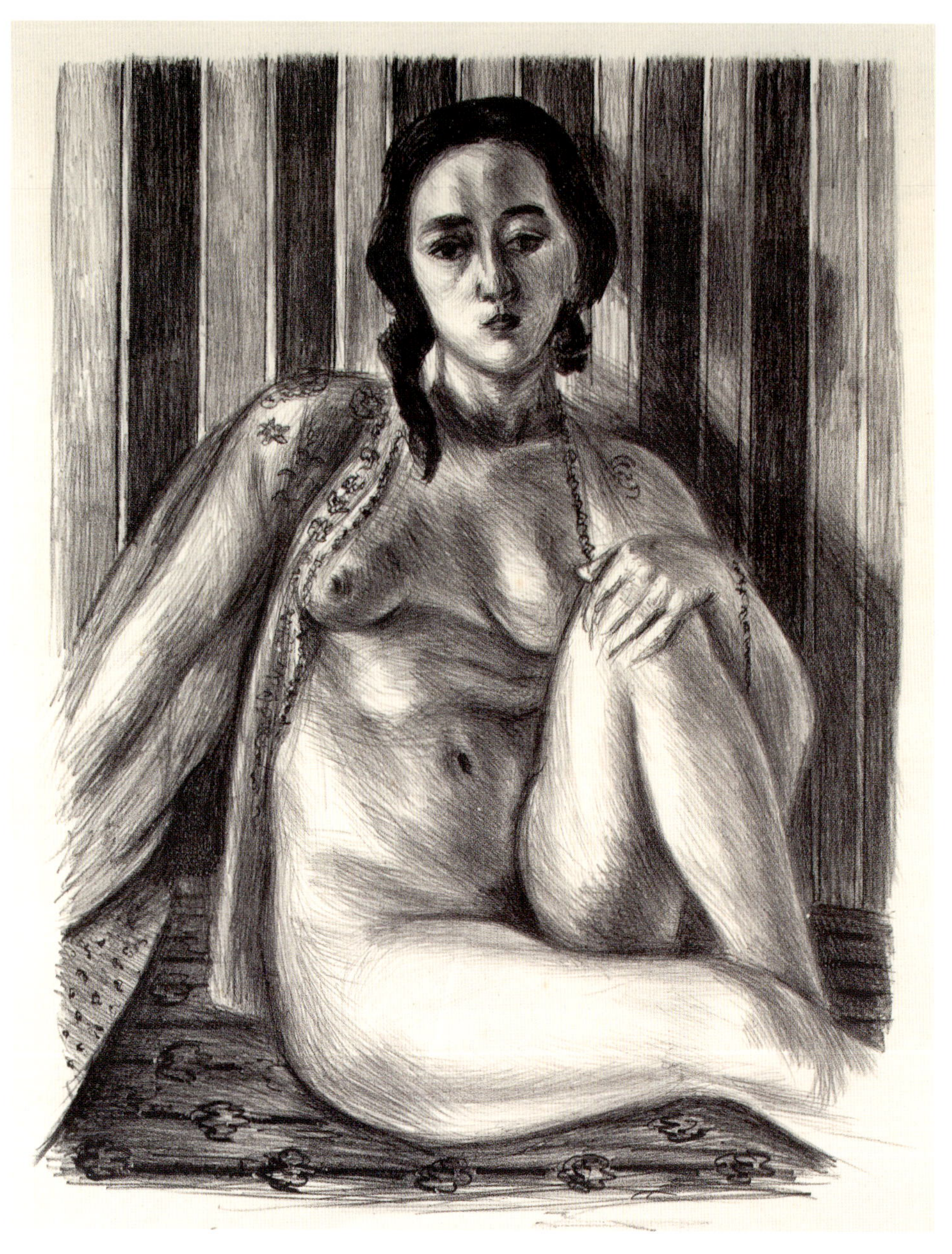

Seated Nude with Tulle Shirt, 1925 (cat. no. 27)

MATISSE: 50 YEARS OF HIS GRAPHIC ART

William S. Lieberman

The following is reprinted from William S. Lieberman, Matisse: 50 Years of His Graphic Art *(New York: George Braziller, 1956), exactly as originally published except for the insertion of my own comments in square brackets.* — JAY MCKEAN FISHER

This book gathers together a selection of Henri Matisse's graphic work produced during a half century. It does not include drawings nor does it attempt a *catalogue raisonné* of his prints.[1] The survey, however, offers a comprehensive review of his work in the many print media he chose to use—drypoint, etching, lithography, linoleum cut, monotype and aquatint. It also reproduces pages from those books Matisse illustrated with original prints. His illustrations for *Jazz,* a brilliant creation of his last years, were conceived to be executed by craftsmen. They are not in any strict sense "originals" but since Matisse directed their entire production they are included here.

Unlike Picasso, Matisse never sustained a continuous level of interest in printmaking. His accomplishment as an etcher and lithographer was prodigious, but it was concentrated into relatively short periods throughout his career. In 1914, for instance, he turned to printmaking with such enthusiasm that surely he sought refreshment from easel painting in the techniques of minor media.

Matisse first worked on copper in 1903. [The actual dates of his first prints cannot be confirmed so are now given the range from 1900 to 1903.] His early prints are tentative essays, the most assured of which, the *Self Portrait as an Etcher* [titled *Henri Matisse Engraving* by Duthuit; cat. no. 1] offers a factual reflection of the artist's image at the age of thirty-three. The other plates are frankly exercises, drypoint studies of a woman in street costume, a half dozen sketches of the nude [see cat. no. 2]. Matisse's casual approach is exemplified by one etching in which heads of the artist's son and daughter accompany a pair of views of the same nude [see cat. no. 3].

In 1906 Matisse composed his first lithographs and linoleum cuts.[2] [These are now known to be woodcuts, not linoleum cuts; see cat. nos. 4, 5, and 6.] The lithographs number twelve, the linoleum cuts three.[3] With one exception—a sketch of the harbor at Collioure [Museum of Modern Art, New York], which he presented to Gertrude Stein—the subjects are either heads of women, or full figures drawn standing, seated or crouching. There is little in these nudes to titillate the erotic sensibility of the spectator. The poses are somewhat unflattering, even distorted, and the series has often been described as *fauve*. Actually the prints are more reminiscent of Matisse's sculpture than of his painting [see cat. no. 8].

After a lapse of several years Matisse returned to printmaking in three media: within a few months in 1914 he produced nine or ten lithographs, at least fourteen monotypes and some fifty etchings. As nudes the lithographs seem somewhat more seductive than the earlier series of 1906 [see cat. nos. 10 and 11]. The designs are free, large,[4] and the attitudes more elegant. The placement of the figure in relation to the printed sheet is arresting: details of the torso are isolated and swept into the rhythm of Matisse's line.

The monotypes of 1914 offer a greater variety of subjects: nudes and, in addition, portraits, still lives and interior scenes [see cat. nos. 14 and 15]. Meticulously printed, probably from copper plates, each is of course unique. Matisse is reported to have been "very much pleased with those prints of his of white lines on a black background."[5]

One may be a self portrait, and all but one are reproduced here. Matisse made no monotypes after 1914.

The etchings of the same year are much more intimate than the lithographs or monotypes. Mostly portraits of friends and family, they build a brilliant sequence of quick and informal characterizations: the wives of the painters Galanis and Gris,[6] Mme Vignier and her daughter Irène, Yvonne Landsberg,[7] the artist's wife and children, and—surprising to a student of Matisse's art—several men, among them the Spaniards Massia, Iturrino and Olivares [cat. no. 12], the British museologist Matthew Stewart Prichard and the American painter Walter Pach [see cat. no. 13].

The portraits were finished with astonishing speed after careful consideration of the sitter. The drawing is quick and decisive. Like all of Matisse's etchings, each is distinguished by its simplicity. Individual features are reduced to vivid details, and often the contours of the face fill the rectangular frame of the copper plate. The figure is treated at greater length only occasionally. Several friends sat more than once, and in the series there are as many as seven different likenesses of the same individual. Only one professional model seems to have posed, "Loulou," who appears head, front and back.

To the gallery of miniature portraits Matisse added a few studies of the nude and a sketch of foliage.[8] He had originally intended to gather the portraits as an album; but instead the etchings were issued separately in editions of five to fifteen proofs each.

Walter Pach has written a lively account of Matisse as a print portraitist in 1914.[9] One October morning in Paris the two had been "talking art" for several hours. Pach looked at the time and said:

"I didn't know it was so late. I have an appointment and must be off in less than ten minutes."

"I'd like to do an etching of you."

"Fine. When shall I come?"

"I'll do it right now. I have a plate ready."

"But I've got to meet M. Hessel for lunch. I've got to leave in five minutes..."

"All right. I'll do it in five minutes."

Matisse placed his watch on the table, set to work and within five minutes outlined the drawing on the plate.

"This isn't serious. I got interested in what you were saying about Rembrandt, and I wanted to set down an impression of you then and there. But come on Sunday morning and we'll have time for a real one."

When Pach returned, he found the etching already printed. There were a few tiny, unimportant spots from "foul" biting of the etching acid. Matisse said, "I did not do those. God did. What God does is well done: it is only what men do..."

Pach sat again and for three hours Matisse sketched other plates. But, the American remembers, "we looked at the little five-minute etching ... it had just the life that the more heavily worked things had lost."

Matisse's first prints, cumulatively significant as a graphic production, were the lithographs, monotypes and etchings of 1914. During the next decade Matisse etched a few plates but not until 1922 does he seem to have resumed working on stone. He began with some hesitation, but in 1925 alone he printed more than twenty lithographs. The most notable is a progression of seated figures which reaches a climax in two large versions of a nude in an armchair and culminates in the voluptuous *Odalisque in Striped Pantaloons* [titled *Large Odalisque with Bayadère Culottes* by Duthuit; cat. no. 23].

Between 1926 and 1930 Matisse increased his yearly manufacture of lithographs. The subjects of some sixty prints are paid models nude or draped. They appear singly,

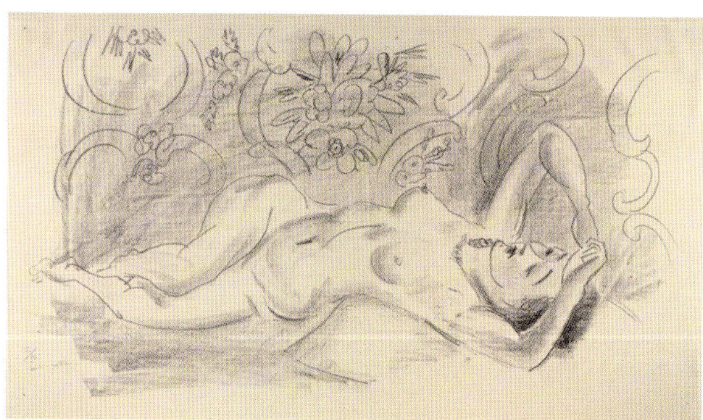

FIG. 1
Henri Matisse, *Reclining Odalisque, Head Down Against Decorative Background*, 1926. Crayon-transfer lithograph, 17 x 31 in. The Baltimore Museum of Art; The Cone Collection (BMA 1950.12.188). © 2008 Succession H. Matisse/Artists Rights Society (ARS), New York

frequently surrounded by accessories of flowers, fabrics or furniture. Matisse's drawing varies from spontaneous studies in line to strongly modeled, meticulous delineations. Sometimes the pose is conventional, sometimes radically contorted. Occasionally the model is seen from above and the arabesques formed by the accessories and figure merge into one fluid pattern.

In his definitive *Matisse: His Art and His Public,* Alfred H. Barr, Jr., concisely summarizes the production of 1926–30. The lithographs "reflect to some degree the reaction toward the bolder, more experimental spirit which generally marks the painting and sculpture of that period. The brilliant outline portrait of the pianist Alfred Cortot is the most striking print of 1926–27 but the very large, fluently drawn and delicately modeled *Reclining Odalisque* [titled *Reclining Odalisque, Head Down Against Decorative Background* by Duthuit; fig. 1] is more characteristic.

"Most of the lithographs published in 1927 are devoted to a new subject for Matisse—the ballet dancer—inspired perhaps by his renewed contact with Diaghilev...."[10] In this series, most of which was issued in the portfolio *Dix Danseuses,*[11] the ballerina

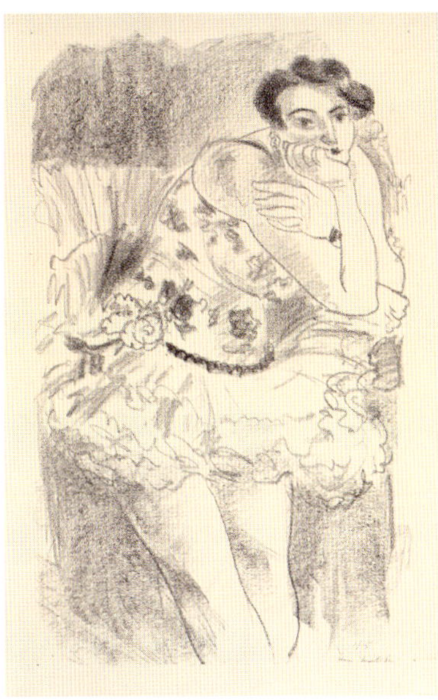

Fig. 2
Henri Matisse, *Ballet Dancer, Resting on Elbows, Seated,* 1925–26. From the series "Ten Dancers," published 1927. Lithograph, 19 5/8 x 12 3/4 in. The Baltimore Museum of Art; The Cone Collection (BMA 1950.12.243). © 2008 Succession H. Matisse/ Artists Rights Society (ARS), New York

is conventionally costumed.... Matisse draws her standing, seated or reclining but, curiously, never dancing or practicing at the bar.... [see fig. 2].

"Possibly Matisse published no stones in 1928 but the twenty or so lithographs of 1929 cover subjects which appear in his painting of 1928.... More than half the lithographs ... are studies of the model seen from various angles as she reclines on a couch surrounded by patterned textiles, flowers, the familiar brass stove, and the Louis XV table....

"The most remarkable lithographs ... are without question the vivid, sharply modeled compositions in which details ... are more elaborately rendered than in any other mature works of Matisse. In the *Odalisque in a Tulle Skirt,* the transparent texture of the garment, the inlay of the Moorish chair and tabouret are precisely simulated not only in the detail but in color values.... *The White Boa* [titled *The White Fox* by Duthuit; fig. 3], a portrait study of the same model, is equally remarkable for its almost photographic effect of light, color and texture but, on close inspection, one finds that the detail has been suggested with extraordinary economy."[12]

Suddenly, at the end of the decade, Matisse resumed etching. Within a few months he produced a constellation of about one hundred and twenty-five plates, studies of nudes and odalisques, and a series of girls gazing at goldfish [see cat. nos. 31–36]. Again, as in 1914, Matisse worked directly on the plate from the model. Sometimes, like the lithographs, the etchings repeat or anticipate motifs in his painting. Usually, although often similar in subject, they remain distinct.

At first this series of etchings may seem incidental but, freshly examined, it reduces daring syncopations of a pose or movement into an essential of lines. Matisse plays endless variations on the same themes. The concise reductions of the etchings of 1929 dispel the still and heavy atmosphere of the seraglio which permeates the lithographs of the late 20s. Matisse's line is lively and inquisitive as it dances out the tensions and balances which sustain the series.

After 1930 Matisse's principal energies as a printmaker were devoted to the illustration of books.

In any discussion of modern French painters as illustrators, it must seem surprising that Matisse and Ambroise Vollard never joined in collaboration. In 1900, with the publication of Bonnard's lithographs to Verlaine's *Parallèlement,* Vollard had established the archetype of books illustrated by artists of the School of Paris. During the next four decades he remained their foremost publisher.[13]

Although Vollard will be remembered as an editor of fine books and prints, his livelihood depended upon his activities as a picture dealer. Among the first to show and sell the paintings of Cézanne and Picasso, he also sponsored Matisse's first one-man exhibition.[14] Their association was brief. A collaboration might have produced a magnificent book, but perhaps Matisse found Vollard too difficult and dilatory an impresario. His only contribution to the publisher's ventures was a single etching delivered for a proposed portfolio of nudes.[15]

At the age of sixty-three when Matisse completed his first illustrated book, most of his younger contemporaries had filled many such commissions.[16] Indeed, in the library of illustrations by artists of the School of Paris, only a volume by Matisse was lacking.[17]

It was a young and courageous Swiss publisher who launched Matisse in his tardy debut in 1932. The previous year Albert Skira had presented Picasso's etched illustrations to Ovid's *Metamorphoses*. Skira's second volume was to be equally distinguished. He asked Picasso's stellar rival to illustrate the poems of Mallarmé. Matisse responded with enthusiasm.

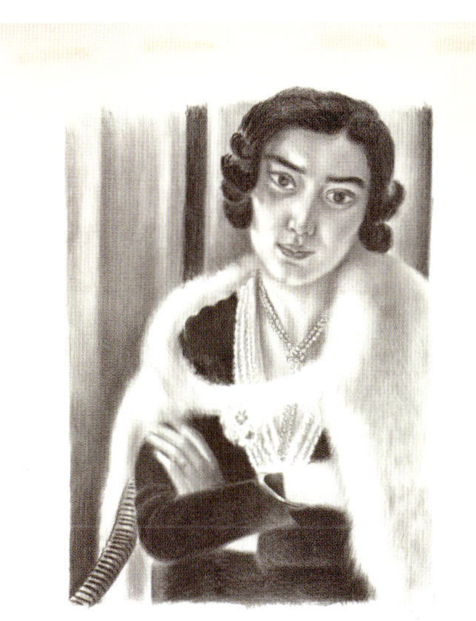

Fig. 3
Henri Matisse, *The White Fox*, 1929. Crayon lithograph, 20 x 14 ½ in. The Baltimore Museum of Art; The Cone Collection (BMA 1950.12.319). © 2008 Succession H. Matisse/Artists Rights Society (ARS), New York

"This is the work I have completed after reading Mallarmé with pleasure.... The drawing is not massed toward the center as usual but spreads across the entire page. The problem was to balance each pair of facing pages—the one with the etching white, the other with the typography relatively black. I achieved this by modifying my arabesques in such a way that the spectator's attention would be interested as much by the entire page as by the promise of reading the text."[18]

The subject matter of the twenty-nine illustrations, like that of the poems themselves, varies considerably. The flowing alternations of Matisse's draughtsmanship, however, lend a continuity and create a deceptive effect of effortless spontaneity. Matisse chose the point of a sapphire for his etching needle which, by its very precision, imposes a quick irrevocable line. Some designs make casual reference to his Tahitian voyage of 1930; others recall earlier figure compositions [see fig. 4]. Never literal, each illustration evokes in a vivid graphic image a specific title or phrase. Longer poems, such as "L'Après-midi d'un faune" and "Hérodiade" are treated at greater length. The most memorable illustration, one of unaccustomed psychological intensity, is the portrait which accompanies the sonnet "Tombeau de Baudelaire [fig. 5]."[19]

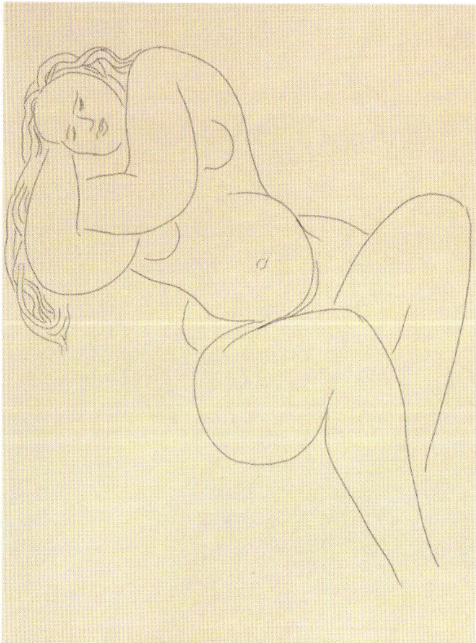

FIG. 4
Henri Matisse, *Tristesse d'été*, 1931–32. Plate 8 from the book *Poésies de Stéphane Mallarmé,* published 1932 by Albert Skira et Cie. Etching, 13 x 19 3/4 in. The Baltimore Museum of Art; The Cone Collection (BMA 1950.12. 691). © 2008 Succession H. Matisse/Artists Rights Society (ARS), New York

A second commission for book illustration was arranged by long-distance telephone.[20] For $5000 Matisse agreed to supply six etchings for an edition of James Joyce's *Ulysses*. The volume was designed by the late George Macy and published for his Limited Editions Club in New York in 1935. In comparison with the Mallarmé, Matisse's contribution was slight and, as illustration, unsuccessful. He was perhaps aware of the parallel construction between *Ulysses* and the *Odyssey*.[21] At any rate he chose to illustrate Homer rather than Joyce.

Five encounters of Ulysses are represented: Calypso, Aeolus, Polyphemus, Nausicaä, Circe and, for the homecoming, a view of Ithaca. The designs were drawn through paper onto a soft ground which covered the copper plates to be etched. This allowed Matisse to delineate as well as to shade as if with crayon or charcoal. In the book, each etching is accompanied by two to five preparatory sketches. The preliminary drawings come to life in a way the finished prints do not. For sheer readability, the double columns of the Limited Editions text may be the most satisfactory presentation of *Ulysses*. But as the illustrator Matisse did justice neither to Joyce nor to himself.[22]

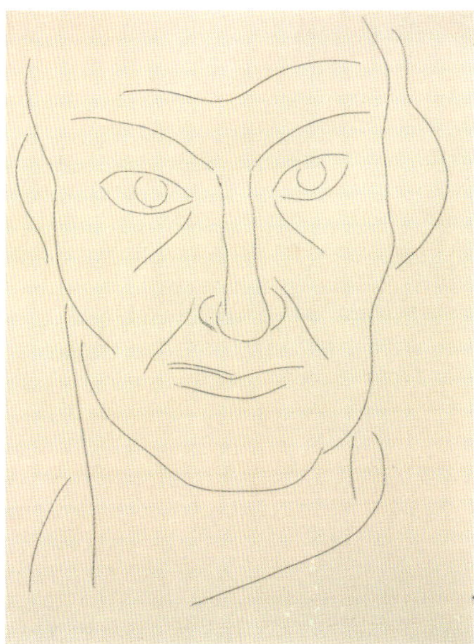

FIG. 5
Henri Matisse, *Le Tombeau de Charles Baudelaire*, 1931–32. Plate 27 from the book *Poésies de Stéphane Mallarmé*, published 1932 by Albert Skira et Cie. Etching, 10 13/16 x 9 9/16 in. The Baltimore Museum of Art; The Cone Collection (BMA 1950.12.691). © 2008 Succession H. Matisse/Artists Rights Society (ARS), New York

During the 30s Matisse continued to print a few etchings and lithographs each year, but his activity as a printmaker never exceeded the prolific production of 1914 or the late 20s [see cat. nos. 45 and 47]. By 1935 he had made some two hundred intaglio plates, three linoleum cuts, almost a hundred and fifty lithographs as well as the early suite of monotypes. He had also completed commissions for two illustrated books. Printmaking had allowed him to distill or elaborate in other media themes on which he had been working as a painter. With fresh inspiration, particularly in illustration, printmaking had expanded the iconography of his art as well.

After 1941 a series of major operations left Matisse an invalid, and he devoted a major part of his time to book illustration. Martin Fabiani, a former associate of Vollard,[23] managed to become a successful dealer during the German occupation of France and, in 1944, published Matisse's third illustrated book.[24] The text consists of extracts from Henry de Montherlant's *Les Crétois*.

The painter and the writer had met in Nice in the winter of 1937. Montherlant sat for his portrait and Matisse considered illustrating his *La Rose de Sable*. "It became necessary to abandon this project. Each time an image began to form in my mind, the end of the story would stop me. Montherlant's description was thorough and complete. I could add nothing." Soon after, however, Matisse did undertake to interpret two selections from *Les Crétois:* "Pasiphaé," a play in verse,[25] and "Chant de Minos," a poem.

For the *Pasiphaé-Chant de Minos* [see fig. 6], Matisse returned to one of his favorite graphic media, linoleum cut. These blocks, however, differ radically from those of 1906. [We now know the 1906 prints were woodcuts.] Instead of carving away to leave a design in relief which prints as black, Matisse retained most of the linoleum's surface. The solid black rectangle of the uncut surface serves as a background to the engraved composition it contains. When inked the incised line of the design prints as white.

Somewhat fussily Matisse cautions: "The lino should not be used as a cheap substitute for wood because it gives to a print its own special character, quite different from woodcut, and therefore should be studied. The gouge is controlled directly by the sensibility of the engraver. Indeed this is so true that the least distraction during the execution of a line causes a slight pressure of the fingers on the gouge and influences the drawing for the worse. Engraving on the linoleum is a true medium for the painter illustrator."

Once again Matisse expands suggestions from a poet's verse into his own personal imagery. The result is more studied than the Mallarmé and Matisse took great care in the composition of the book as a whole. "A single white line on an absolutely black background.... The problem is the same as for the Mallarmé, but the two elements are reversed. How to balance the black page without text with the comparatively white page of typography? ... by bringing together the page engraved and the page of type ... a wide margin surrounding both pages completely masses them together.... I had a definite feeling of a somewhat sinister character of a book in black and white. However, a book generally seems like that. But in this case the large page almost entirely black seemed a bit funereal. Then I thought of red initials.... Starting out with capitals that were picturesque, fantastic, the inventions of a painter, I was obliged to change to a more severe and classic conception of lettering in keeping with the elements of typography and engraving already chosen.... So then: Black, White, Red—not so bad."

Matisse's enthusiasm for linoleum cut was not satisfied by the illustrations to Montherlant alone. He incised about two dozen other prints—heads of women and

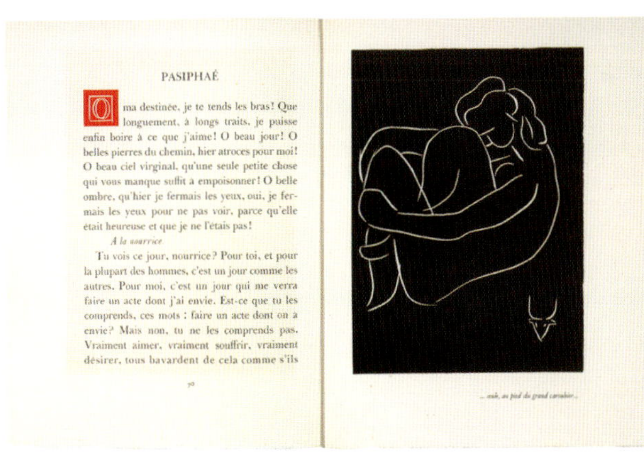

PASIPHAÉ

O ma destinée, je te tends les bras! Que longuement, à longs traits, je puisse enfin boire à ce que j'aime! O beau jour! O belles pierres du chemin, hier atroces pour moi! O beau ciel virginal, qu'une seule petite chose qui vous manque suffit a empoisonner! O belle ombre, qu'hier je fermais les yeux, oui, je fermais les yeux pour ne pas voir, parce qu'elle était heureuse et que je ne l'étais pas!

A la nourrice

Tu vois ce jour, nourrice? Pour toi, et pour la plupart des hommes, c'est un jour comme les autres. Pour moi, c'est un jour qui me verra faire un acte dont j'ai envie. Est-ce que tu les comprends, ces mots : faire un acte dont on a envie? Mais non, tu ne les comprends pas. Vraiment aimer, vraiment souffrir, vraiment désirer, tous bavardent de cela comme s'ils

70

FIG. 6
Henri Matisse, *Seule au pied du grand caroubier...*, 1943–44. Plate 13 and text from the book *Pasiphaé, Chant de Minos*, published 1944 by Martin Fabiani. Linoleum cut, 12 7/8 x 9 3/4 in. The Baltimore Museum of Art; The Cone Collection (BMA 1950.12.744). © 2008 Succession H. Matisse/Artists Rights Society (ARS), New York

still lives of fruit [see cat. nos. 48–50]. Again, in 1952, he would produce another series of independent prints, but between 1941 and 1950 his principal activity as a printmaker continued to be illustration. Often he was at work on several projects at the same time and their order of publication does not necessarily follow their sequence of composition.

A certain pedestrian sameness characterizes Matisse's next four volumes—*Visages, Repli,* a *Lettres Portugaises* and a *Fleurs du Mal,* all begun in 1943 and 1944 and issued during the winter of 1946–47. The author of *Visages,* Pierre Reverdy, was a friend of Matisse. So was André Rouveyre, the caricaturist and author of *Repli,* who lived at Vence where Matisse had moved in 1943.[26] Both books contain some dozen lithographs of heads as well as ornaments cut in linoleum.

For Efstratios Tériade,[27] like Skira a leading publisher of fine editions, Matisse adorned the five letters of the Portuguese nun, a dependable inspiration for artists good and bad. Matisse supervised the entire layout. The lithographs, charming if repetitious, offer a profusion of initials and leaves printed in violet, and a sequence of portraits of the cowled epistolarian herself.

A Baudelaire by Matisse should have been an important publishing event. It was not. The artist conceived *Fleurs du Mal* with more than thirty lithographs and twice as many wood engravings. Dry weather unfortunately ruined the transfer paper on which Matisse had drawn. Finally the illustrations, mostly female heads, were photographed and mechanically reproduced. They bear little affinity to the passion of the poems. A portrait of Baudelaire reaffirms that Matisse's tribute to the poet had been the earlier, stark and abbreviated mask for Mallarmé's sonnet.

During the composition of *Visages, Repli, Lettres Portugaises* and *Fleurs du Mal,* Matisse was devoting his best energies to three other books. The first, *Jazz,* was published by Tériade [see fig. 7]. The illustrations are not original prints but splendid color reproductions of designs Matisse worked out with scissors, paste and pins.[28] He composed *Jazz* during a twelve months' confinement to his bed in 1944. When the book was issued in 1947, he appeared not only as illustrator but as author as well.

In the fall of 1941 Skira had visited Matisse in Nice. The painter spoke of a project he had often considered, an illustrated anthology of Ronsard's love poems. The book was planned to contain some thirty lithographs to be printed in Switzerland. The first printing of the text did not suit Matisse's illustrations, so a new type face was selected, a font of rather worn Caslon. A second proof of the text was pulled for Matisse's use in making the illustrations. The war delayed another meeting until 1946. The artist had so expanded the original plan that when the Caslon was shipped from Geneva to Paris it had to be reset for a third time. After eight months the text pages were ready for the printing of the illustrations. But again misfortune struck. The sheets had turned yellow, the edition had to be scrapped, the Caslon type was too worn to be used again. After a long search Skira found William Caslon's original molds and a new font was cast. Matisse meanwhile had changed the color of the ink and had quadrupled the number of illustrations. The fourth and final printing was not made until the spring of 1948—seven years after the project had been initiated.

The love lavished upon the Ronsard is apparent as one turns its pages [see fig. 8]. The format is large and handsome. To his own choice of poems Matisse drew one hundred and twenty-six lithographs printed in brown on an off-white paper. In the Ronsard, unlike the Mallarmé or the Montherlant, Matisse does not stress a left-hand right-hand balance between text and illustration. The two are composed together. A

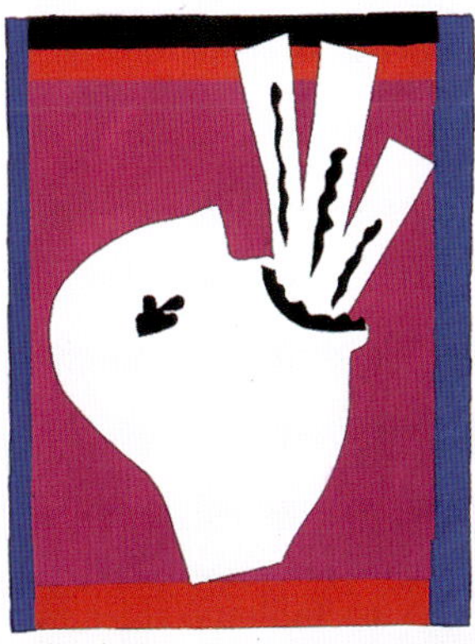

Fig. 7
Henri Matisse, *The Sword Swallower*, 1943–47. Plate 14 and text from the book *Jazz*, published 1947 by Tériade. Text, lithograph, illustration, and color stencil *(pochoir)*, 16 9/16 x 12 3/4 in.
The Baltimore Museum of Art; The Cone Collection (BMA 1950.12.745).

scene of a woman bathing under a willow covers an entire folio; a pattern of leaves lightly embroiders a double spread of text pages; female heads, fragments of a nude, flowers, fruit, decorate other pages of poems; larger full-page illustrations suggest in a few sure lines scenes of pastoral romance, the reverberations of a kiss, the silhouette of a vase, the song of birds. The conception of each page is fresh and unexpected, as lyric and graceful as the poems themselves.

After this tribute to Ronsard, Matisse made an elaborate bow to another poet, Charles d'Orléans [see fig. 9]. In a large notebook of a hundred pages Matisse penned forty poems and ornamented the manuscript with color crayons. As an introduction, the first four pages are covered with fleurs-de-lis, the royal emblem of France chosen by Charles' grandfather. A gay title page in blue and red faces a noble profile portrait of the author. The fleurs-de-lis motive is thereafter repeated on each left-hand page. The lilies of France vary in size, number and arrangement. The leaves themselves are drawn in two colors, the combination changing with each page. Opposite these fields appear the various rondels, ballads and songs. On the right-hand pages Matisse copied the courtly verses in pen and ink and framed each poem with a witty rococo border. Five

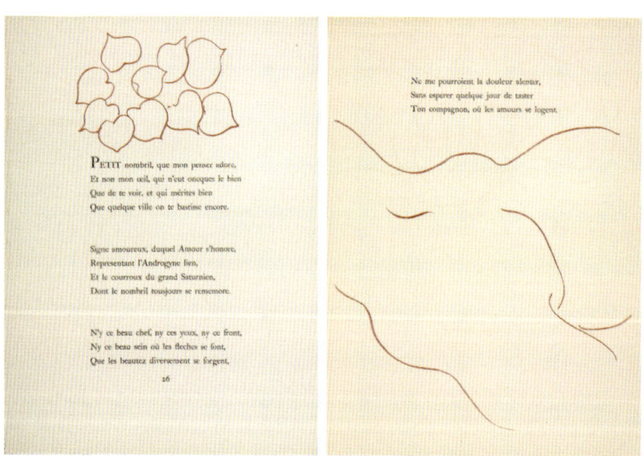

Petit nombril, que mon penser adore,
Et non mon oeil, qui n'eut onoques le bien
Que de te voir, et qui mérites bien
Que quelque ville on te bastisse encore.

Signe amoureux, duquel Amour s'honore,
Representant l'Androgyne lien,
Et le courroux du grand Saturnien,
Dont le nombril tousjours se rememore.

N'y ce beau chef, ny ces yeux, ny ce front,
Ny ce beau sein où les flesches se font,
Que les beautez diversement se forgent,

26

Ne me pourroient la douleur alenter,
Sans esperer quelque jour de taster
Ton compagnon, où les amours se logent.

Fig. 8
Henri Matisse, *Petit nombril, que mon penser adore…*, 1941–48. Pages 26 and 27 from the book *Florilège des amours de Ronsard*, published 1948 by Albert Skira et Cie. Lithograph, 15 3/16 x 11 9/16 in. The Baltimore Museum of Art; The Cone Collection (BMA 1950.12.743). © 2008 Succession H. Matisse/Artists Rights Society (ARS), New York

times the pages are interrupted by illustrations—three portraits of women, a meadow of rabbits and a nude enshrined in a flower.

It is impossible not to share Matisse's lighthearted pleasure in the creation of this book. He delights in teasing his ingenuity as far as possible within the arbitrary limits of the fleurs-de-lis foliates. The brightly colored illuminations are elegant, playful and extravagant.[29]

The *Poèmes de Charles d'Orléans* is the last of eight illustrated books Matisse completed during the decade of the 40s. During the winter of 1951–52 he returned to printmaking as such and drew an important series of about twenty aquatints.[30] These consist mostly of women's heads freely brushed onto the plate to create, when printed, the effect of bold drawings in ink [see cat. nos. 53–58]. He also signed a few lithographed sheets which could be sold for the profit of the Dominican Nuns of Vence whose chapel he had constructed and decorated [see cat. no. 62].

Book illustration was an endeavor admirably suited to Matisse's last years. During his increasingly prolonged confinements in bed at Nice, Vence, Paris and then Nice again,

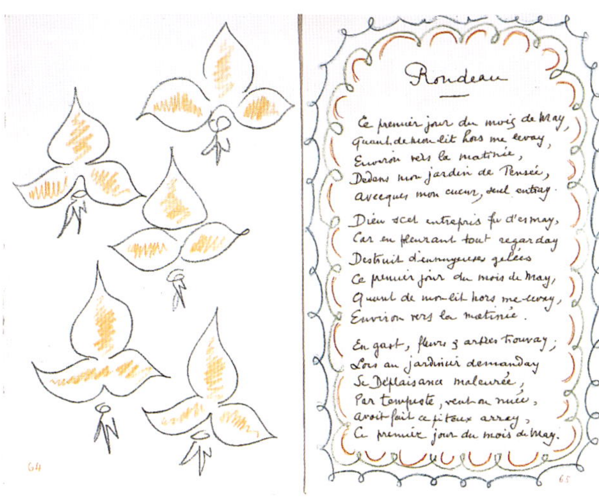

Rondeau

Ce premier jour du mois de May,
Quant de mon lit hors me levay,
Environ vers la matinée,
Dedens mon jardin de Pensée,
Avecques mon cueur, seul entray.
Dieu scet entrepris fu d'esmay,
Car en pleurant tout regarday
Destruit d'ennuyeuses gelées
Ce premier jour du mois de May,
Quant de mon lit hors me levay,
Environ vers la matinée.
En gast, fleurs & arbres trouvay;
Lors au jardinier demanday
Se Desplaisance maleurée,
Par tempeste, vent ou nuée,
Avoit fait ce piteux arrey,
Ce premier jour du mois de May.

FIG. 9
Henri Matisse, *Fleurs-de-lis, and border with Rondeau,* 1943–50. Pages 64 and 65 from the book *Poèmes de Charles d'Orléans,* published 1950 by Verve. Lithograph, 16 ¼ x 10 ¼ in. The Baltimore Museum of Art; Gift of the Artist (BMA 1951.236).

he could easily spread before him the materials and texts for his projects. Illustration demanded less physical exertion than painting, and peace of mind and contentment characterize the presentation of *Jazz*, the Ronsard and the Charles d'Orléans.

When supported by an enthusiastic publisher such as Skira or Tériade—expense and time cannot be considered—Matisse had no rival as an illustrator.[31] He responded most readily to his favorite authors and believed that "the artist to make the most of his gifts must be careful not to adhere too slavishly to the text. On the contrary he must work freely, his own sensibility enriched through contact with the poet he is to illustrate.

"I do not distinguish between the construction of a book and that of a painting, and I always work from the simple to the complex, yet always ready at any moment to reconceive in simplicity.... Put your work back on the anvil twenty times and begin over again until you are satisfied."

The past six decades have witnessed a development in printmaking so extraordinary that today fine prints have assumed an unprecedented importance. Never before have so many of the foremost painters of any period devoted so much of their best energies to the production of original prints.

Recently there has been a revived enthusiasm for work in color, while in size prints themselves have outgrown the confines of the collector's portfolio. This increasing emphasis on color and scale has been encouraged by the public—today most prints are produced and purchased not for study but for prominent display on the walls of homes and museums.

Matisse, however, remained faithful to the custom of black and white, nor is the size of any of his single prints excessive. Only in illustration, in his last years, did he essay color and it must be remembered that the sheets for *Jazz* are no more than meticulous reproductions of his original collage designs.

Picasso, Rouault and Villon sustained a continuous interest in printmaking throughout their careers. Matisse did not, and perhaps his graphic oeuvre is less varied and less important in relation to his painting. But his accomplishment in black and white, limited though it may be to specific moments during a half century, is a brilliant example of the tradition of *peintre graveur.*

Notes to the Text

1 For several years Matisse's daughter, Mme Georges Duthuit, has been preparing a definitive catalog of her father's prints. Mr. Carl O. Schniewind, Curator of Prints and Drawings at the Art Institute of Chicago, has also established a working catalog of Matisse's graphic oeuvre. Details as to paper and *tirage* should properly await the publication of their compilations. Both Mme Duthuit and Mr. Schniewind have generously allowed the author to examine their notes. [The Duthuit catalogue was eventually published in 1983 in two volumes. A third volume dedicated to the illustrated books was published by her son, Claude Duthuit, in 1988. The Schniewind manuscript, never published, is now in the archives of the Art Institute of Chicago.]

2 The print [cat. no. 7] reproduced on page 8 has often been called Matisse's first lithograph and has been dated as early as 1904. The year 1907, assigned by Christian Zervos, *Cahiers d'Art,* vol. 6, no. 5–6, 1931, p. 92, seems more likely. [The lithograph is now dated in the Duthuit catalogue raisonné as 1906.]

3 In the summer of 1948 Mme Matisse told the author that she herself had cut the three linoleum cuts of 1906. Her husband, she said, drew the designs on the linoleum and then supervised her carving. [There must have been confusion here as the existence of a block for *The Large Woodcut* definitively establishes that the matrix was a wood block rather than a sheet of linoleum; fig. 4 of Fisher essay, present volume.]

4 The lithographs of 1906 are printed on sheets of paper measuring, most frequently, 17 ¾ x 10 ¾" (451 x 273 mm). Those of 1914 on sheets 19 ¾ x 13" (502 x 330 mm).

5 Albert Clinton Landsberg, in a letter to Alfred H. Barr, Jr., quoted in his *Matisse: His Art and His Public,* New York, Museum of Modern Art, 1951, p. 541, note 4.

6 For many years Josette Gris, wife of the painter, has been a close friend of the Matisse family. Gris was often in need of money and Mme Gris posed for Matisse several times. She is characterized in seven of the etchings of 1914.

7 Matisse etched five likenesses of Yvonne Landsberg, perhaps most famous for her painted portrait now owned by the Philadelphia Museum of Art. For the circumstances of several portraits see Barr, *op. cit.*, pp. 184–5.

8 An etching of the Pont St. Michel has sometimes been assigned to 1914. It was published however by Emile-Paul Frères, *Tableaux de Paris,* Paris, 1927.

9 Walter Pach, *Queer Thing, Painting,* New York, Harper & Brothers, 1938, pp. 219–20.

10 The Matisse-Stravinsky ballet *Le Chant du Rossignol,* first produced by Diaghilev's Ballets Russes in 1920, had been revived, with new choreography, in the spring of 1926.

11 *Dix Danseuses,* an album of 10 lithographs, published by the Editions de la Galerie d'Art Contemporain, Paris, 1927.

12 Mr. Barr's monograph, *op. cit.*, is and probably will remain the authoritative discussion of Matisse's life and work. It contains much information concerning the painter as a printmaker and has been freely consulted here.

13 At the time of his death, he had issued volumes with illustrations by Bonnard, Rodin, Séguin, Bernard, Denis, van Gogh, Dufy, Picasso, Degas, Rouault. He had also contracted, although not published, illustrations by Redon, Roussel, Vuillard, Maillol, Derain, Braque, Segonzac, and Chagall.

14 The exhibition took place in Vollard's crowded gallery in the rue Lafitte, June 1–18, 1904.

15 The Vollard album of nudes, never published, was initiated about 1927. It was to have included prints by Bonnard, Chagall, Dufy, Forain, Maillol, Matisse, Picasso, Rouault and others. Editions of these prints were pulled during Vollard's lifetime and have since been individually distributed. Matisse's contribution was an etching, 7 13/16 x 11 11/16" (198 x 297 mm): a reclining odalisque in pantaloons; she wears a necklace and her hands are folded behind her head.

16 Matisse had presented prints or drawings to four books before 1932. These are in no sense illustrations, but contributions to volumes compiled by friends. Barr, *op. cit.*, pp. 559–60.

17 Other picture dealers had followed the example of Vollard. Daniel Henry Kahnweiler, for instance, issued volumes illustrated by the painters Derain, Picasso, Vlaminck, Braque, Léger, and Gris. Dufy's woodcuts to Apollinaire's *Le Bestiaire* appeared as early as 1911; Maillol's woodblocks to Virgil in 1926.

18 Quotations from the artist are taken from: 1) "Montherlant vu par Matisse," *Beaux-Arts,* August 27th, 1937 [subsequently published in Flam, *Matisse on Art,* pp. 127–29]; 2) Henri Matisse, "Comment je fais mes livres," *Anthologie du livre illustré* edited by Albert Skira, 1944 [subsequently published in Jack Flam, *Matisse on Art,* pp. 166–68]; 3) Henri Matisse, *Jazz,* Paris, Editions Verve, 1947; 4) Adelyn D. Breeskin, "Swans by Matisse," *Magazine of Art,* October, 1935.

19 "The complete maquette for these illustrations is now a part of the Cone collection. Included in the group are

over 60 drawings, 52 etchings and 29 cancelled etching plates."—Adelyn D. Breeskin, Director of the Baltimore Museum of Art. Most of the preliminary drawings for the etchings appear on the pages where the text has already been printed.

20 See Barr, *op. cit.*, p. 249.

21 It seems probable that Matisse discussed the construction of *Ulysses* with his literary friends. He was acquainted with many avant-garde writers including, of course, his son-in-law Georges Duthuit.

22 In his statement "Comment je fais mes livres," *op. cit.*, Matisse does not even list *Ulysses* among his illustrated books.

23 A collaboration with Vollard was no longer possible. He had died in 1939. It is possible, however, that Vollard in 1937 had instigated the meetings between Matisse and Montherlant in view to a possible publication.

24 Fabiani, the previous year published *Dessins: Thèmes et Variations*, several series of pencil drawings by Matisse gathered together and reproduced as a de luxe edition.

25 *Pasiphaé* was first produced in Paris at the Théâtre Pigalle on December 6, 1938.

26 In 1918 Matisse had contributed five drawings to Pierre Reverdy's *Les jockeys camouflés et période hors-texte;* in 1912 he drew a portrait of Rouveyre which was used as a frontispiece in a monograph by Louis Thomas.

27 Tériade, as the publisher of *Verve*, frequently reproduced Matisse's paintings and several issues of the magazine bear covers designed by the artist.

28 Matisse first covered sheets of white paper with thin washes of brilliant colors. Then he cut out figures and forms. These he arranged into designs and the "drawings with scissors," as Matisse called them, were reproduced by *pochoir* (stencil) using the same colors the artist himself had mixed.

29 In *Vignt ans d'activité*, 1948, Albert Skira has written an account of the publication of *Florilège des amours de Ronsard.*

30 Tériade published the *Poèmes de Charles d'Orléans* in 1950. Priced inexpensively as if to emphasize its popular appeal, twelve hundred and thirty copies were printed—about four times as many as in the usual de luxe edition.

31 Since Matisse preferred to make his illustrations while a book was actually in progress, it is doubly fortunate that he had the best possible technical collaboration. Most of his illustrations were printed in Paris by Roger Lacourière for the etchings, the brothers Mourlot for the lithographs. The knowledge, patience and understanding of these master printers contributed substantially to the success of his best volumes.

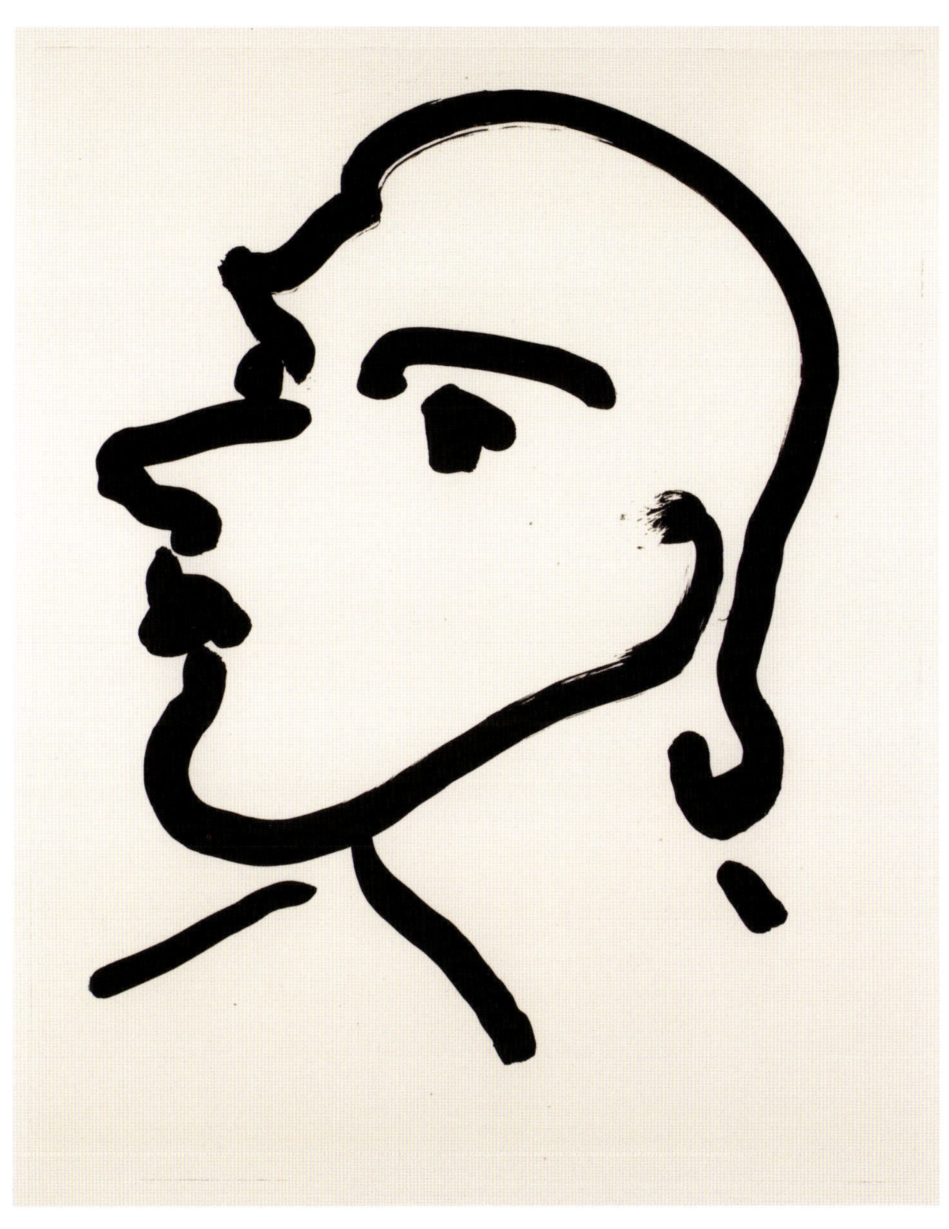

NADIA IN PROFILE, 1948 (cat. no. 57)

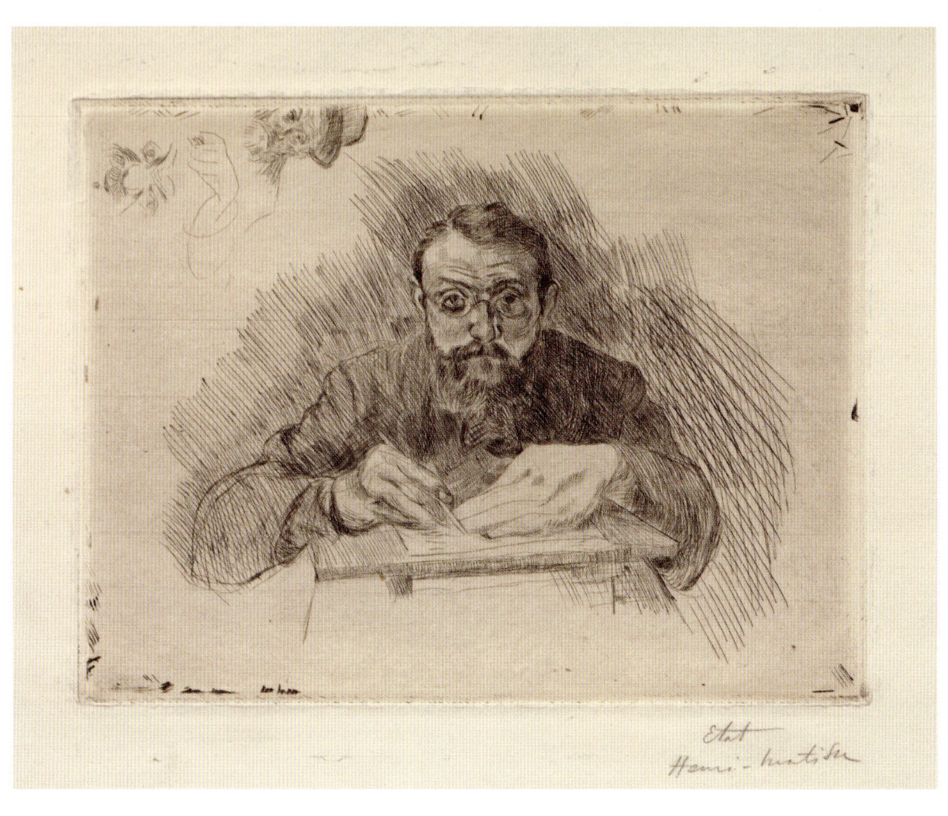

Henri Matisse Engraving, 1929 (cat. no. 1)

HENRI MATISSE–BUT WHY PRINTMAKING?

Jay McKean Fisher

What motivated Matisse to make prints? He wrote eloquently and demonstrated both as a teacher and by the example of his own art how important it was for an artist to pursue multiple approaches to creative expression—painting, sculpture, drawing. Yet no clear statement from him about the intrinsic value of printmaking is known.[1] It seems obvious, however, that he saw printmaking as an extension of drawing, which he made clear was central to his art.[2] To view Henri Matisse's prints is to encounter his drawing, and through the chronology of his prints we learn how his approach to drawing changed and functioned in different modes. He made prints fairly consistently from 1900 until his death in 1954. We see in them the same elemental process of observation that we find in his drawings, the process through which he transformed what he saw into his art.

Matisse's printmaking oeuvre amounts to an enormous visual library, a published record more accessible and complete than any of his drawings assembled for exhibition could offer. For an artist so committed to revealing his process of creation, printmaking, as a means of making multiples, was essential, and he exploited it throughout his career. Just as it had for artists in the centuries before him, it gave him a way to distribute his art to many more collectors than could ever acquire his unique works. Through deft collaboration with collectors, Matisse became quite adept at marketing his art, and as enthusiasm for his work grew in the United States and Europe, he produced more prints and illustrated books.[3] His printmaking oeuvre comprises more than eight hundred images, often in editions of twenty-five or fifty each. The multiple prints included in his illustrated books bring the total to well over ten thousand published prints.[4] Matisse shared this prolific print production with contemporaries such as Pablo Picasso, Joan Miró, and others of his generation.[5]

What is it about the making of prints, and the degree of priority Matisse gave them within his production, that may show us the nature of his interest in them? As William Lieberman observed, Matisse, unlike Picasso, had no deep engagement in the technical aspects of printmaking.[6] He was not stimulated by an active, firsthand engagement with printmaking methods; working in etching, aquatint, monotype, lithography, woodcut, and linoleum cut, he used what was available, and his technical approach was fairly straightforward. His interests in making prints were wide-ranging, however, and innovative as a result. Through the power of his vision, he found ways to exploit the various print techniques, and he was always open to learning from professional printers. This is perhaps most evident in his involvement with transfer lithography, where instead of using standard transfer papers he drew on a variety of drawing papers with different textures—the distinct "tooth" in the "wove" paper surface resulting in variations in the character of the lines that were carried through to the printed images. Matisse would work with these variations in technique in a serial manner, something only evident upon close examination of the prints themselves.[7] The intimate view of printmaking that we see in his early self-portrait at work (cat. no. 1), which visually recalls Rembrandt's etching of himself drawing at a window (fig. 1), presents an image of Matisse as the toiling printmaker, the dedicated craftsman. An aura seems to emanate from his hands, as if they were acting instinctively in the realization of his ideas. Like any traditional etching or drypoint, the print evolved laboriously through several states. Matisse would become a very different kind of printmaker in the future. This drypoint self-portrait, like several other prints of 1900–03, is drawn with a needle sharp enough to slice through the surface of the copper plate but only with applied pressure, curtailing the free movement of the hand. These first prints are tentatively drawn, and the plates are filled with added vignettes in different orientations: sketches of family members, models in the studio, or women of the town (see cat. nos. 2 and 3). The prints, then, were the work of an artist trying his hand at a new technique, although the results warranted their production, if in small editions.

Matisse returned to drypoint a decade later, in 1913, but quickly moved on to etching, where instead of pressing hard on his tool to make the lines he had only to draw through a pliable protective coating on the plate. This ground could easily be scraped away with a free hand, baring the metal for the corrosive acid that would do the real work of scoring the lines. Printmaking now became a comfortable activity for Matisse, like drawing, and a casual, even constant aspect of his studio practice. In fact, he installed his own press in his studio, allowing him, as we know from his friend Walter Pach, to work spontaneously on small plates, most often taking up portraits of his family and friends (see cat. nos. 12 and 13).[8] This kind of engagement recalls the early printmaking experiments of Edgar Degas and Camille Pissarro, which were largely isolated from the marketplace—they were social affairs in the studio, within

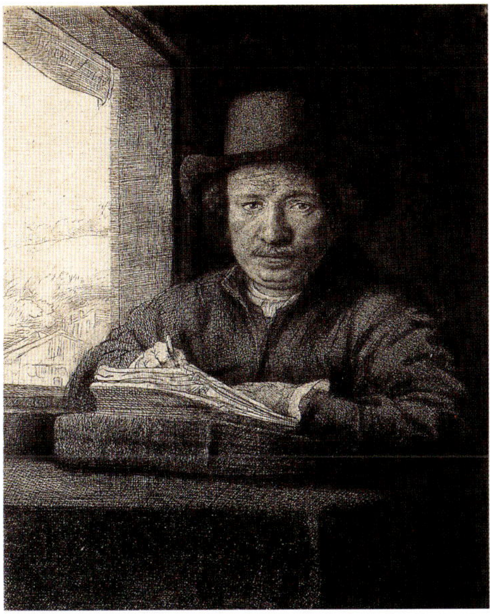

FIG. 1
Rembrandt van Rijn, *Rembrandt Drawing at a Window*, 1648. Etching, engraving, and drypoint, 6 3/16 x 4 13/16 in. The Baltimore Museum of Art; Garrett Collection (1946.112.7779)

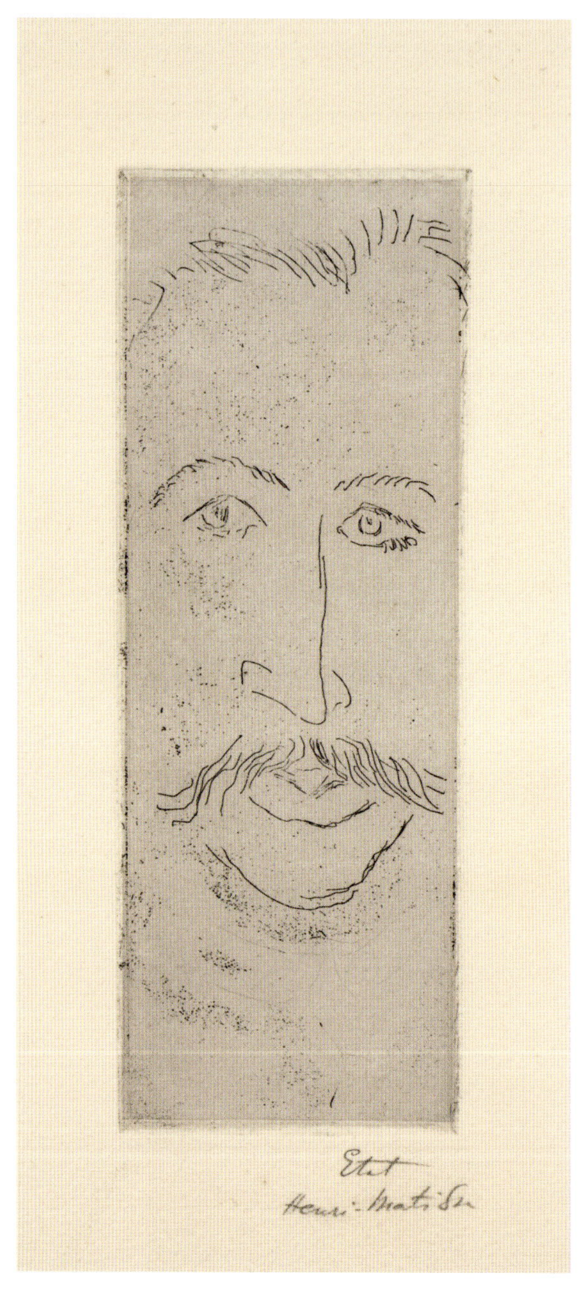

Portrait of Walter Pach, 1914 (cat. no. 13)

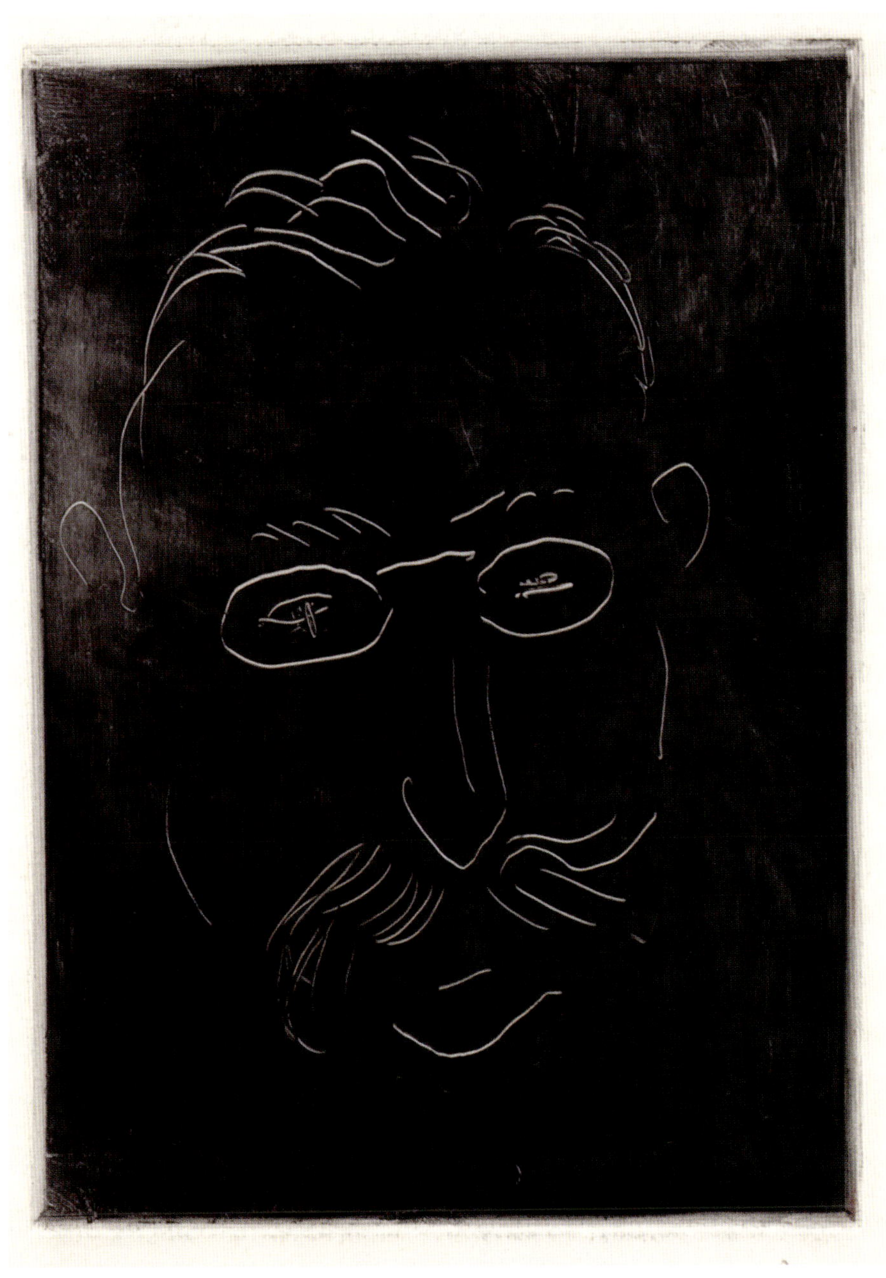

The Painter Albert Marquet, 1914–15 (cat. no. 15)

the secure company of family and friends. The nature of etching encouraged Matisse to take a spare, spontaneous approach using simplified linear drawing. Gone were the short strokes and hatching marks required by the drypoint tool. The etching line became more fluid and nuanced, like a pen line, for Matisse quickly learned to vary the pressure he applied to the etching needle to control the weight and width of the line as he drew. He used plates of various dimensions and proportions—skinny verticals, long rectangles, and squares—and often cropped the image, always conscious of the placement of the composition within the overall dimensions of the plate. Some of these works utilized the chine-collé technique, being printed on a light, tissue-weight paper that becomes adhered to a heavier sheet. Matisse's etched lines had become fragile enough that to be adequately printed they required the receptivity of this lightweight paper. As portraits of friends and family, many of these prints were purposely rapid records of what Matisse observed and sensed about the character of the portrayed.

If we accept that Matisse was not inclined to experiment with printmaking, the most startling exposition of his developing engagement with this art form is a group of nearly seventy monotypes made in 1914–15 (see cat. nos. 14 and 15). The ease with which monotypes could be made, and then the image on the plate wiped away in order to start again, had enticed many artists, such as Degas, to take up the practice. Reportedly with family helping at the small printing press and preparing the inked plates, Matisse simply used a piece of rolled paper or cardboard to draw through dark ink coating the plate, making images that would print as white lines against a dark field. These were one-off prints, with the plate soon wiped clean, ready for another image. If the result was unsatisfactory, the print could be discarded and the image wiped away without a trace, like sheets torn out of a sketchpad. Drawing a line through the pliant ink on the plate was similar to working with a soft graphite pencil on smooth paper. The line could be fluid and spare; the surrounding black brought the viewer's attention to the line, which could swell as it described the contour of a shoulder or become an abbreviated thin mark to suggest a raised eyebrow on a nearly featureless face. These bright lines attracted the light, in luminous contrast to the surrounding, light-absorbent black. While most of Matisse's small monotypes were portraits like his etchings, their subjects also broadened to include figures and still lifes. In their simplicity, and through their demonstration of Matisse's instinctive control of this reductive medium, the monotypes alert us to aspects of his art that he was exploring in the intense and probing phase of his painting during the same period. Although he would make no monotypes after 1917, his later use of the linocut, beginning in 1938, would enable him to return to this linear drawing, now in a medium that allowed the printing of editions.

This casual kind of production was private and exceptional in Matisse's printmaking, for he produced the vast majority of his prints in professional printmaking shops as multiples for collectors. He was particularly prolific in lithography, the most economical way of making print editions. He either worked directly on the stone or used transfer lithography, which allowed him to draw in his studio with no concern for the reversal of the image that occurs when the printmaker works directly on his matrix. It was the master printer who would undertake the challenge of making his drawing a print, but the artist had a clear expectation of what the result would be and was meticulous in the approval proofing required before an edition was printed. Matisse admired the remarkable lithographs of Odilon Redon, probably responding to Redon's command of light and dark. He would equal Redon's mastery of blacks in his lithographs of 1925 (see cat. no. 27), and he understood that such luminous effects could only be achieved by working directly on the stone.[9] For his very first lithographs of 1906, he sought out Redon's printer, the great craftsman Auguste Clot, who worked in Paris and was renowned for techniques that capitalized on the painterly insights but novice printmaking skills of such artists as Pierre Bonnard, Paul Cézanne, and Edouard Vuillard.[10] Clot and artists such as these had together established lithography's reputation as a medium well suited for the new painters emerging in the last decades of the nineteenth century. In availing himself of a professional printer of Clot's standing to make editions of twenty-five impressions each, Matisse demonstrated his confidence in producing prints for sale. It is all the more remarkable that the images he created showed little concern for the tastes of the marketplace: these lithographs were nudes and nothing less than shocking in the willful audacity of their poses and the almost coarse expression of his line. The intention in this group of prints seems to be to bring the viewer into the studio, to experience the artist at work in what he implies to be a single modeling session. The model is directed in a series of thirteen images, showing close-up views of her head and the back and front of her torso, crouching, seated, and head upside-down. Most striking is the character of Matisse's drawn line. For this, the artist exploited the potential of the transfer technique, which allowed him to draw on "wove" papers with noticeable texture that would be faithfully transferred to a plate or stone and then to the printed surface. It was no longer necessary to use special transfer

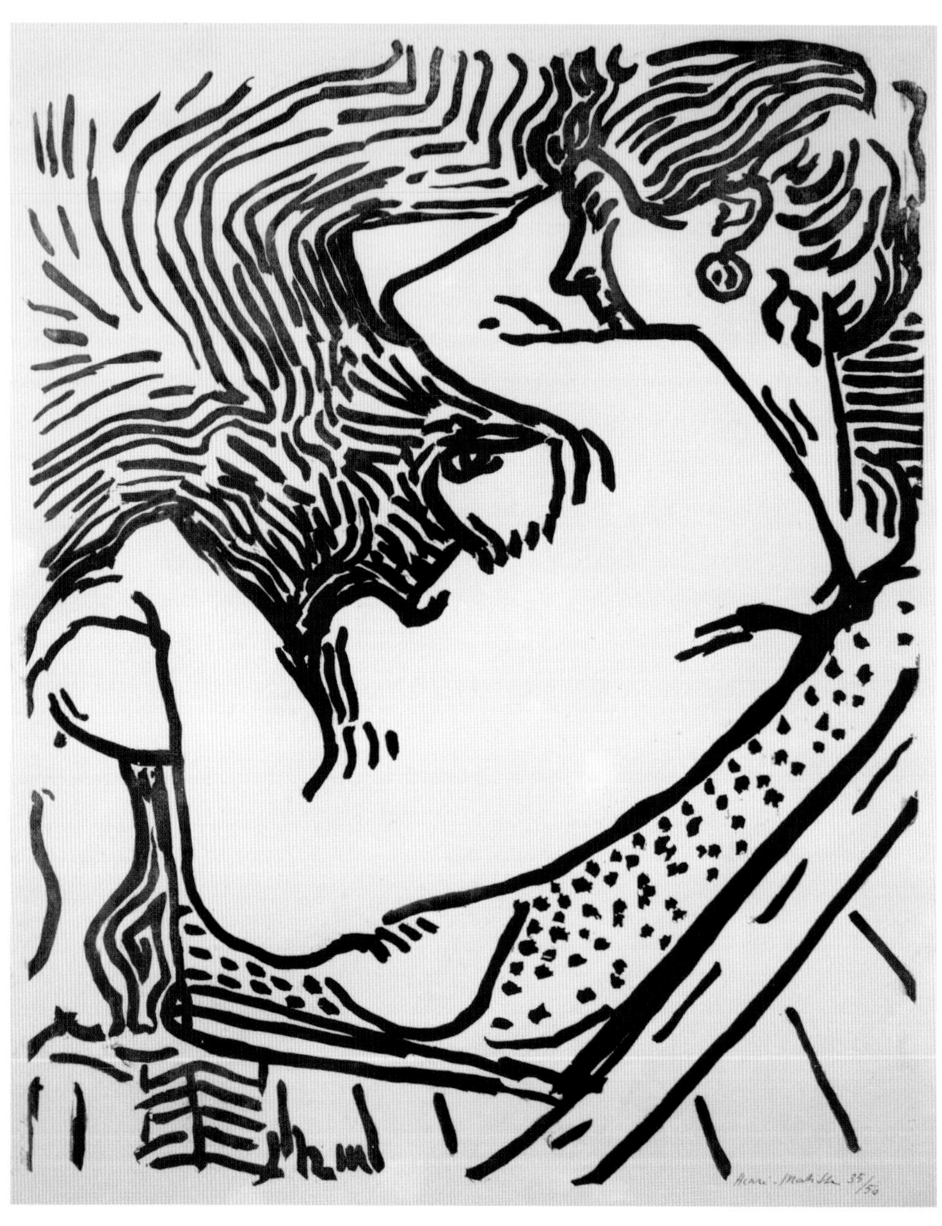

The Large Woodcut, 1906 (cat. no. 5)

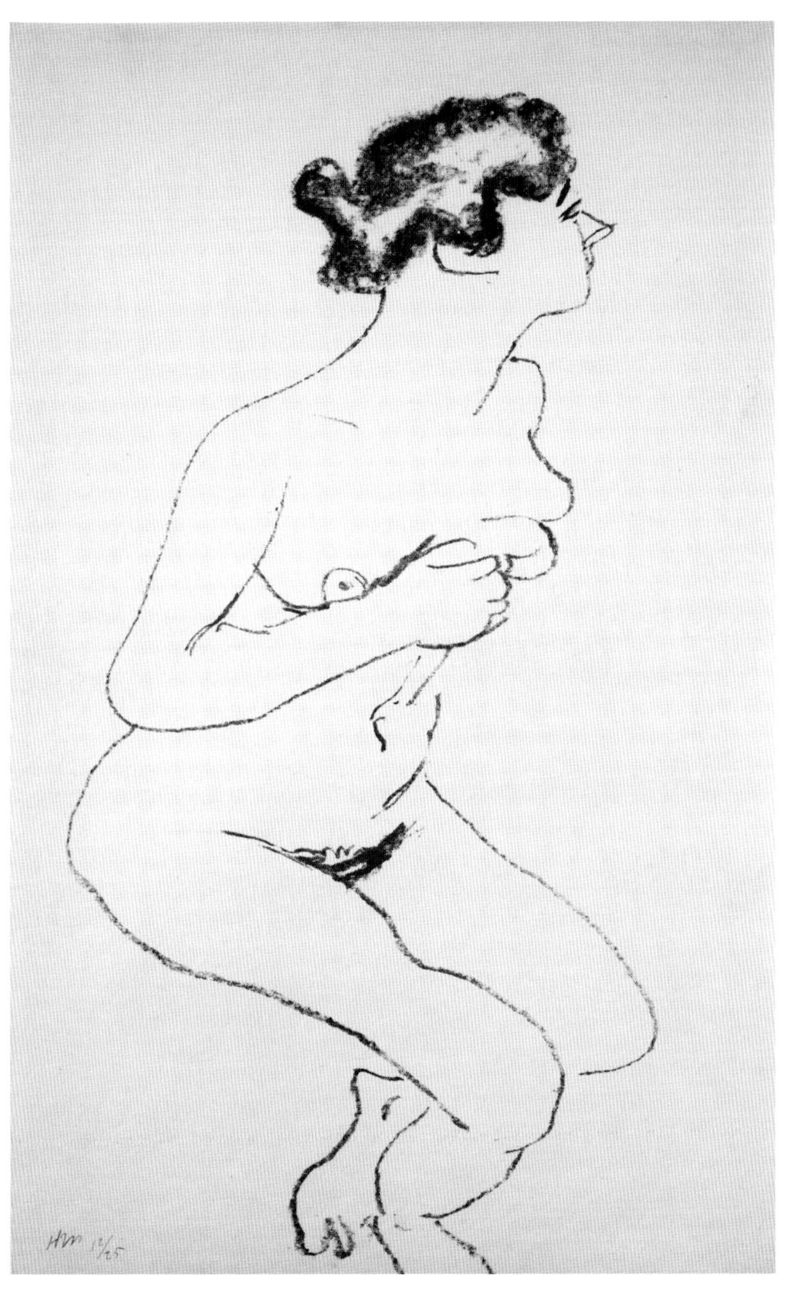

Crouching Nude with Black Hair, in Profile, 1906 (cat. no. 8)

papers. Subsequently, whenever Matisse utilized the linear mode in his printmaking, desiring a direct transcription of the drawn line, he would turn again to the transfer method, using drawing papers of different textures.

These transfer lithographs joined the many drawings and sculptures that Matisse had made while working on major paintings such as *Luxe, calme et volupté* in the winter of 1904–05 and, especially, *The Joy of Life (Le Bonheur de vivre)* (fig. 2) a year later. Some of the lithographs must have been postscripts to that painting, where he returned to a particular pose to develop it further. Though made with the specific purpose of printmaking in mind rather than as preparatory drawings for the painting, the drawings made for transfer as lithographs are characterized by the same linear rhythm that we find in the figural contours in *The Joy of Life*. In the progression of Matisse's drawing style, the prints actually present a new aspect, as John Elderfield states: here "pure continuous line drawing appears in his art for the first time."[11] The prints also alert us to an important aspect of Matisse's composition of the image on the sheet, most apparent in the act of printmaking: the use of cropping to position

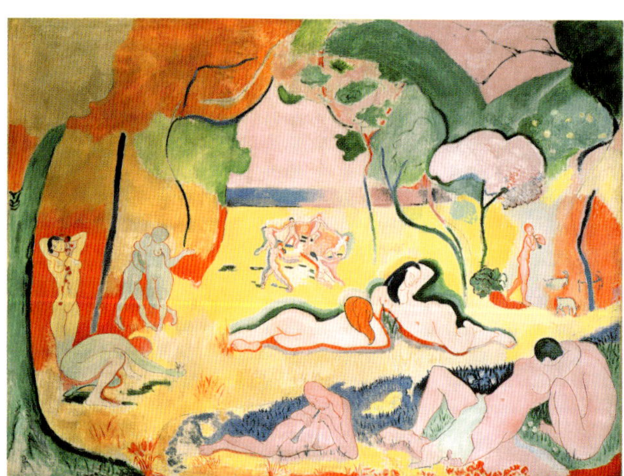

FIG. 2
Henri Matisse, *The Joy of Life*, 1905–06. Oil on canvas, 68 ½ x 79 ¾ in. The Barnes Foundation. © Succession Henri Matisse/ Artist Rights Society (ARS), New York. Photo © The Barnes Foundation/Bridgeman Art Library

the figure in relation to the dimensions of the sheet. This can be seen clearly in the lithograph *Three-quarter View of Nude with Cropped Head* (cat. no. 10), where the shoulder and elbow touch the perimeter of the sheet and the head is cut off at the top edge. For the prints, Matisse chose a warm Japanese paper that claims the space surrounding the figure as part of the image.

Also in 1906, and working with the same model, Matisse produced a series of three woodcuts (cat. nos. 4–6), works in a radically different mode from both the lithographs and the early drypoints. Like the transfer lithographs, these prints began as drawings on paper, which were then transferred to a block and actually cut by the artist's wife, Amélie, with astonishing fidelity to the character of the drawn pen lines (figs. 3 and 4). Given the fluidity of the line, Lieberman mistakenly thought these prints were linocuts, but a surviving block discovered later attests to the use of woodblocks.[12] In the drawing for the woodcut, we can see how Matisse's bold strokes, applied to the paper with a broad reed pen, seem to gouge the paper just as the woodcutting tool has furrowed lines into the block. The artist's mark-making fractur results in an even plane of dark lines against the uniform background of the white paper; modeling through graduated shading is dispensed with, so that every drawn line is uniformly surrounded by the paper's opposing brightness, giving us the visual impression of strong illumination. These brilliant contrasts of black and white radiate the same intensity as the isolated areas of color in Matisse's fauve paintings of the same year. The individualized mark-making recalls the drawings of Vincent van Gogh, who similarly introduced us to a personal language in which we come to perceive that details are signified rather than represented. We can also recognize the influence of Paul Gauguin's distinctive 1890s woodcuts of Tahitian subjects. These unconventional prints, with their "primitiveness" in technique and materials, set the course for a style of fauve woodcuts. The drawings for the woodcuts may have shown Matisse the way to a more expressive approach to contour drawing.[13] More radical and abstract than the 1906 lithographs, they demonstrate what Elderfield has called the central concern of Matisse's drawing in this period: "Matisse, having united linear and decorative plasticity in 1905, is now testing the linear against the decorative in different combinations."[14] Printmaking would be the witness to his exploration of these seminal issues extending from drawing and painting.

In discussing the lithographs, Lieberman suggests, "actually the prints are more reminiscent of Matisse's sculpture than of his painting."[15] What unites the two forms is the immediacy of the sensation that Matisse is at work with the model in the studio, whether drawing with a crayon on paper or modeling wet clay with his hands. The poses have become relaxed and natural, far from the postures of life study in the academic classroom. In both the prints and the sculpture, the figures take positions that anticipate movement, articulating the body in such a way that we feel in the poses the extension and release of muscular tension. In these prints, the use of the white of the paper to signify light suggests the sculptural experience of reading volume through the work of light on the surface of bronze.[16] The striking lithograph *Large Nude* (cat. no. 7), which Lieberman dates to 1904 but which is now generally accepted as 1906, could not be more different from the other prints of 1906, even though it explores the same reclining pose.[17] In this case, Matisse drew directly on the lithograph stone rather than using the transfer process; this allowed him to scrape away the crayon strokes to add shading and highlights, shaping what he had already drawn on the stone. This manner of working on the stone in a planar style parallels his work in sculpture, for example, in *Reclining Nude I (Aurora)* (fig. 5), where the figure is modeled and shaped by the addition and removal of clay.

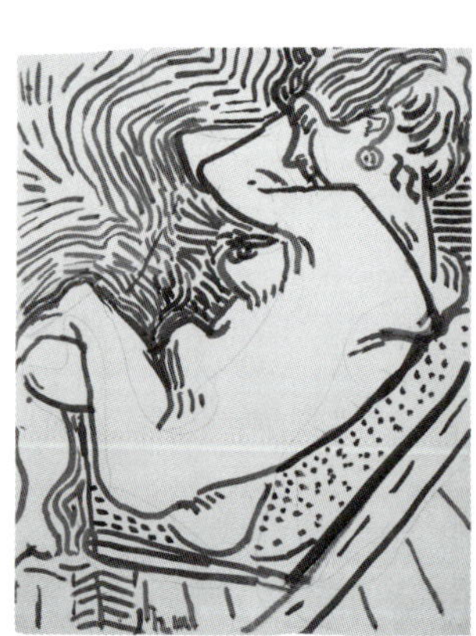

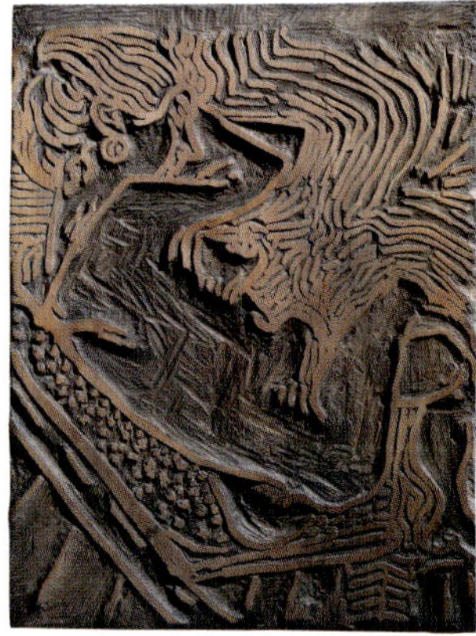

Fig. 3
Henri Matisse, *Seated Woman*, 1906. Brush and ink on paper, 18 1/4 x 14 1/4 in. The Metropolitan Museum of Art; Gelman bequest, 1999 (1999.363.39). © 2008 Succession H. Matisse/Artists Rights Society (ARS), New York

Fig. 4
Henri Matisse, *Block for Large Woodcut*, 1906. Woodblock with residues of blue and white paint, 19 1/2 x 15 3/4 in. Victoria and Albert Museum (V&A E.409-1975). © 2008 Succession H. Matisse/Artists Rights Society (ARS), New York

Alongside the groundbreaking advances in Matisse's painting during these years, his printmaking might be viewed as less than central, a less rigorous, even conservative means of creative relaxation. His second series of eight transfer lithographs in 1913 (see cat. nos. 10 and 11), in which he continued the same serial observation of a single model and again drew in outline, demonstrates the contrary. The style of drawing changed in fundamental ways. What earlier read as exaggerated bodily distortion drawn with thick crayon lines evolved to something more reductive and spare, a line that seems more sensuous and fluid. We again witness the artist at work, but the results, rather than seeming aggressively expressive and suggestive of movement, attest to a more static synthesis of line and form. This style of drawing would be further advanced in the monotypes of 1914–15. Viewing the lithographs and monotypes within the broader context of Matisse's drawings and alongside his paintings of these years, it is possible to see that, while on canvas he was articulating a new interest in abstraction, in drawings and prints he stayed with his navigational reliance on extended observation of the model.

In the last decade, we have come to see more of Matisse's drawings and particularly his working drawings, many separated from sketchbooks, which were never much

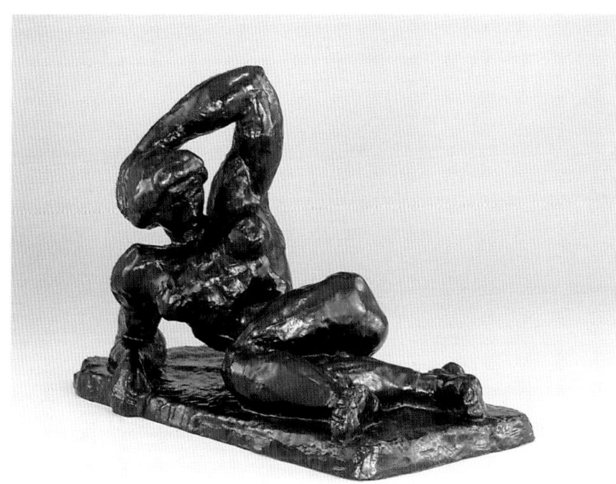

FIG. 5
Henri Matisse, *Reclining Nude I (Aurora)*, original model 1907, this cast ca. 1930. Bronze, 13 9/16 x 19 5/8 x 11 in. The Baltimore Museum of Art; The Cone Collection (BMA 1950.429). © 2008 Succession H. Matisse/Artists Rights Society (ARS), New York

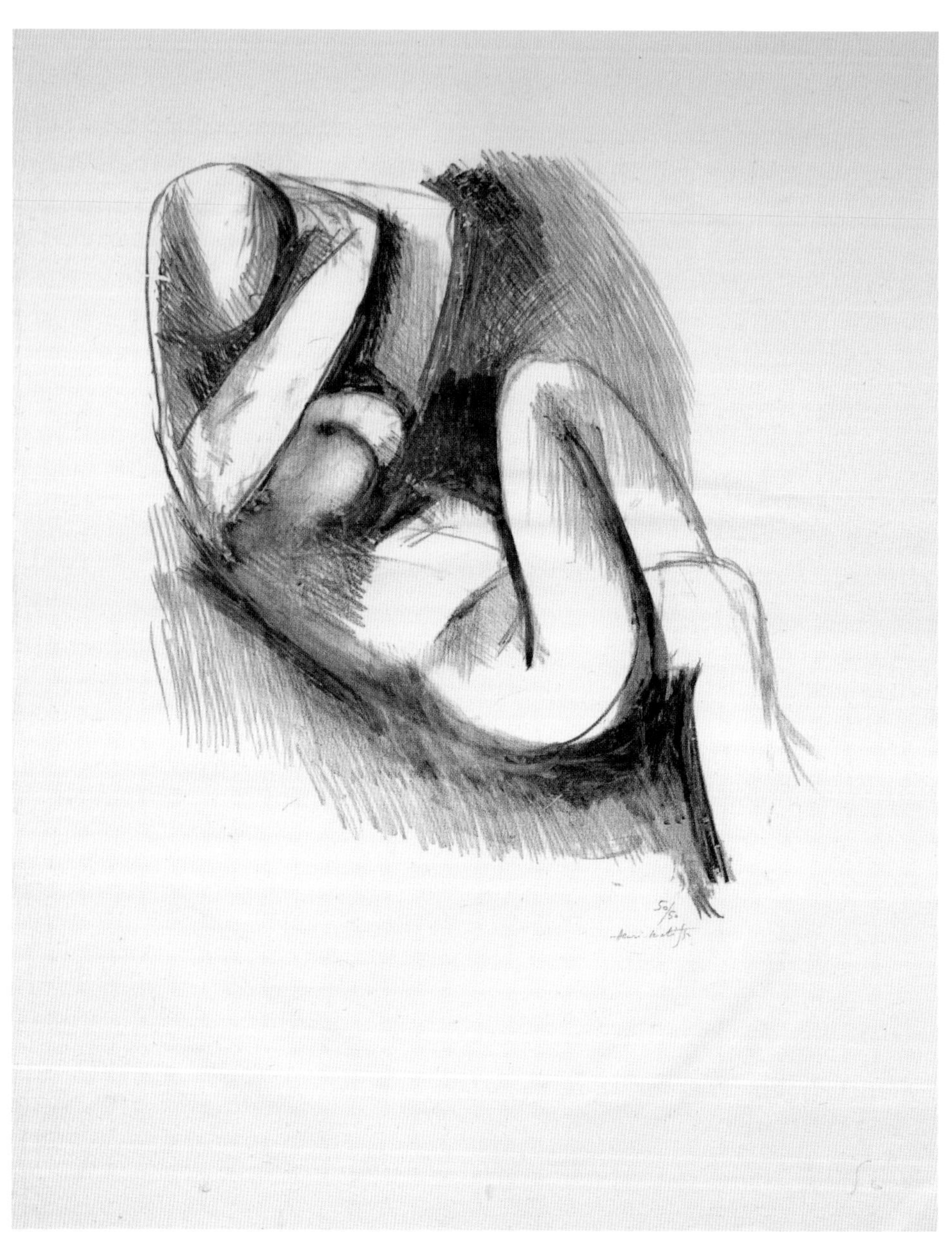

The Large Nude, 1906 (cat. no. 7)

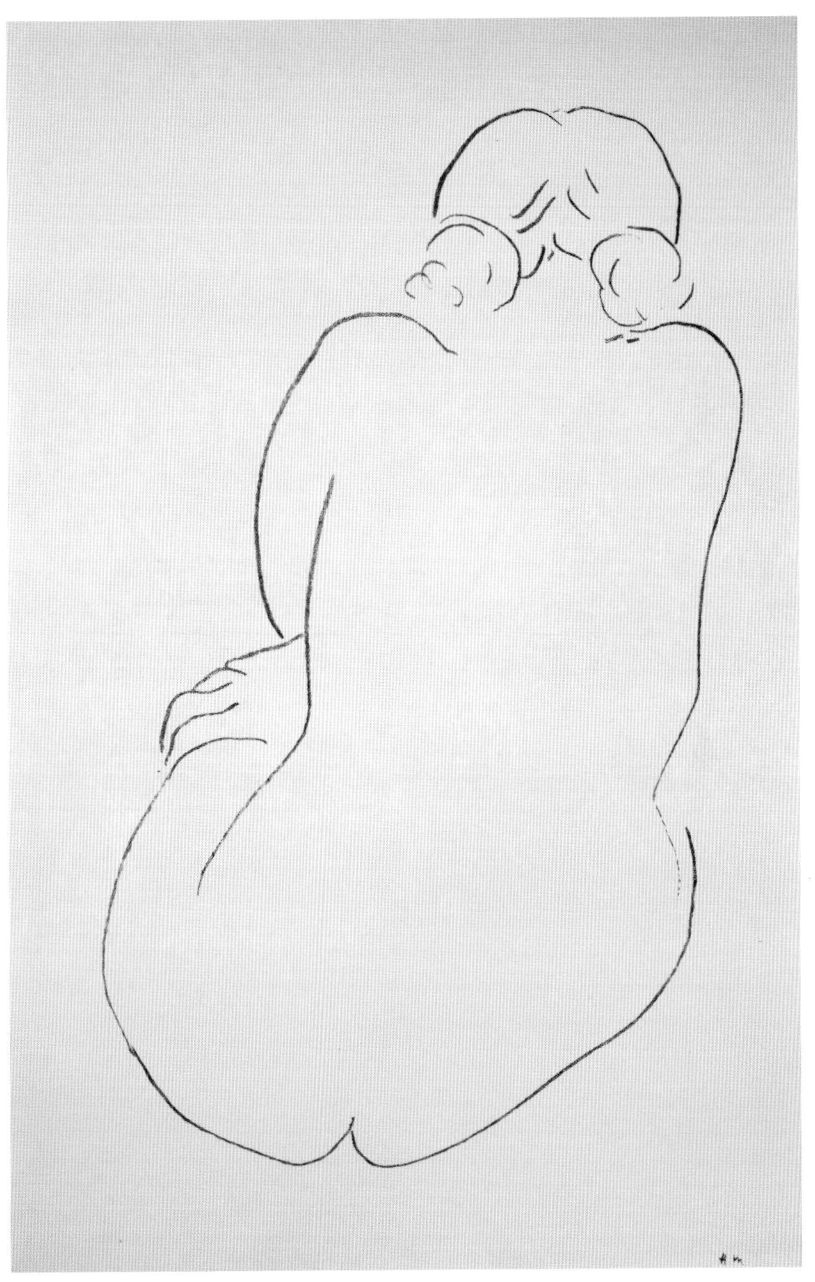

Seated Nude, Viewed from Behind, 1913 (cat. no. 11)

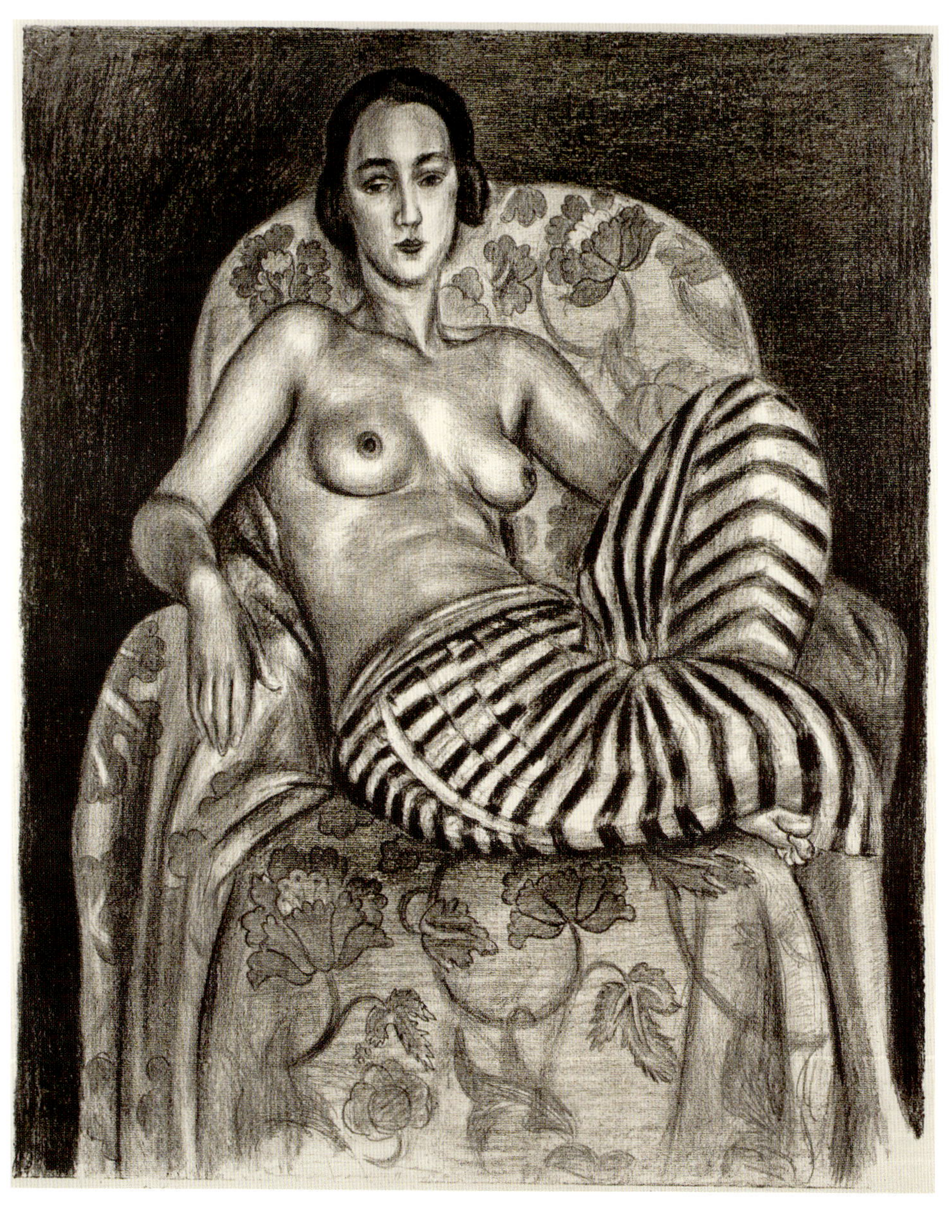

Large Odalisque with Bayadère Culottes, 1925 (cat. no. 23)

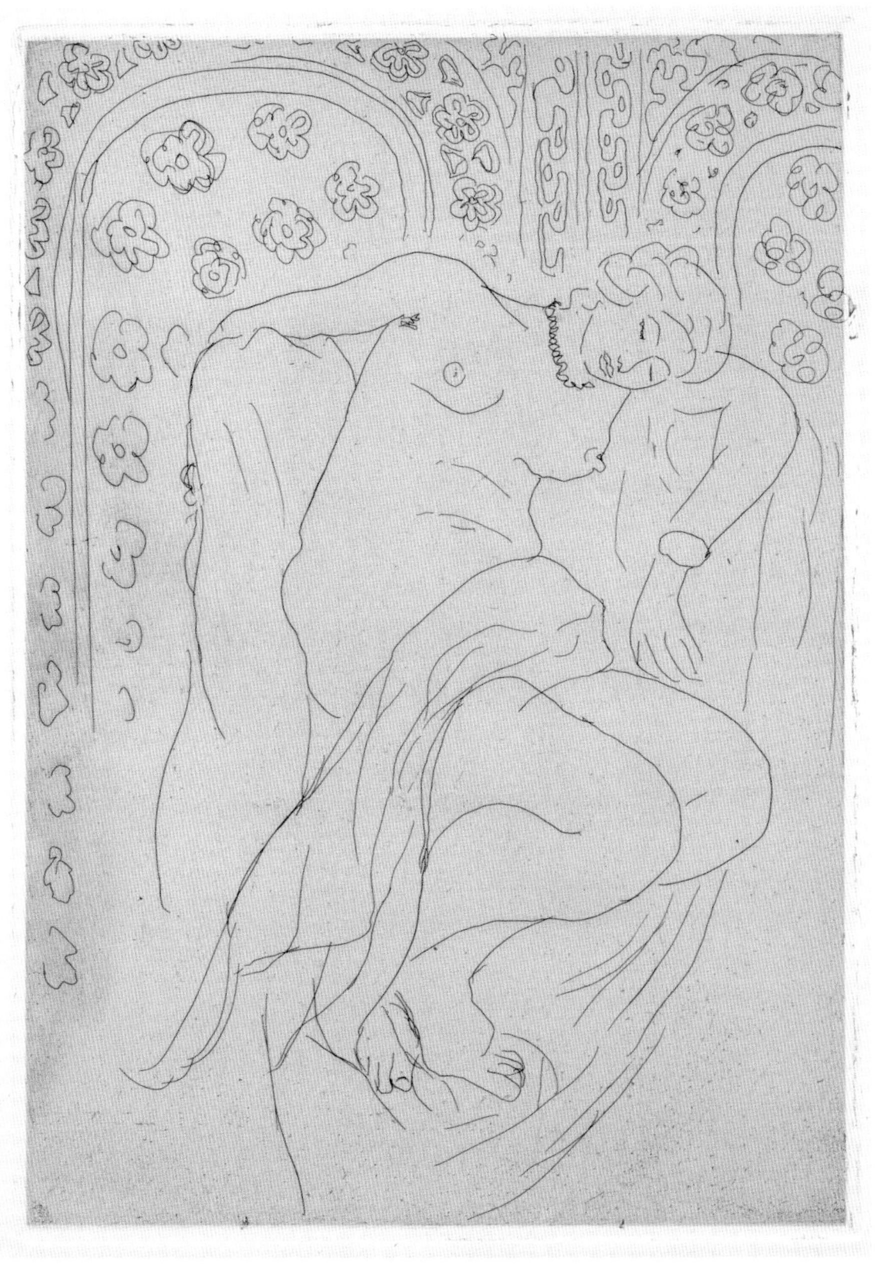

Sleeping Figure in front of a Mashrabiya Background, 1929 (cat. no. 38)

desired by collectors and which he retained for his private use. Consequently, these drawings remained in large numbers within his estate. We are inclined to view the images in the print series similarly, as if they were pages in a sketchbook—work from the studio before a process of selection and refinement. But this is exactly what Matisse's printmaking of this kind was: a process of selection, in which a given drawing was chosen for transfer into lithography. Since he was likely using regular drawing paper rather than dedicated transfer paper, there may be many more drawings that he could have transferred for prints but did not. This author has seen Matisse drawings on paper similar to that used for transfer in the making of lithographs. Although the prints seem to suggest the immediacy of a studio session, they must represent more selective choices that the artist made later, to demonstrate a particular vision—one realized in front of the model and restaged in the prints. Neither of the lithograph series, from 1906 or 1913, suggests a specific sequence, a progressive vision, but when seen together they communicate a continuous flow of observation as the model varies poses, gestures, and attitudes. Each "lithographic drawing" represents a stopping point, a point of resolution, but still a pause in an ongoing process.

Printmaking was Matisse's primary means of demonstrating to his audience his working process, the character of his vision, and the way his drawing transformed what he observed. These prints attest to the necessity of working with the model. Although they are the result of careful selection, they communicate an immediacy in recording sensation and the process through which a different conclusion—a new visual synthesis—is achieved. Prints in series were rarely collected as complete groups, but seeing them this way must have been the artist's preference: the serial nature of his printmaking is basic to their creation, and almost all of Matisse's prints are made in series—a particular mode of drawing, a specific pose, a single model. Indeed, what made Matisse so devoted to the illustrated-book format was that it enabled the artist to publish images in sequence. The organization of Matisse's books is never entirely determined by the text; what is foremost is a visual structure, orchestrated in concert with the typography and the blocks of text. Many of these books have now been disassembled by dealers and collectors, allowing their images to be sold individually and relatively inexpensively—a painful violation of the artist's intentions. In his desire to elucidate his vision by publishing drawings as multiples, Matisse departed from the orthodoxy of "original" printmaking. Instead of making transfer lithographs, for instance, he published photo-lithographic reproductions—facsimiles—of original drawings in carefully produced portfolios printed in large editions, such as the 1920 publication *Cinquante dessins par Henri Matisse* and the 1943 publication *Dessins: Thèmes et variations*.[18] The latter remains the only composite of drawings made in series, as the originals are now mostly dispersed. His second book, an edition of James Joyce's *Ulysses* commissioned by an American publisher and completed in 1935, traces the process the artist followed in conceiving the six soft-ground etchings that illustrate the book. Each of these plates is followed by a series of drawings reproduced on colored papers as facsimiles of the originals.[19]

We know little about the economics of Matisse's print production or how successfully his prints sold during his lifetime, except that many remained in his estate at the time of his death. The significance of this is limited, however, since his production was prolific, and until the last few decades, the prices for his prints remained relatively low. After the monotypes of 1914–17, he made few if any prints until 1922, when a print publisher commissioned him to make a lithograph, *Model Resting* (cat. no. 16), to be printed in a large edition. Matisse's patronage broadened during the 1920s, and, not surprisingly, his print production increased dramatically: between 1922 and 1930

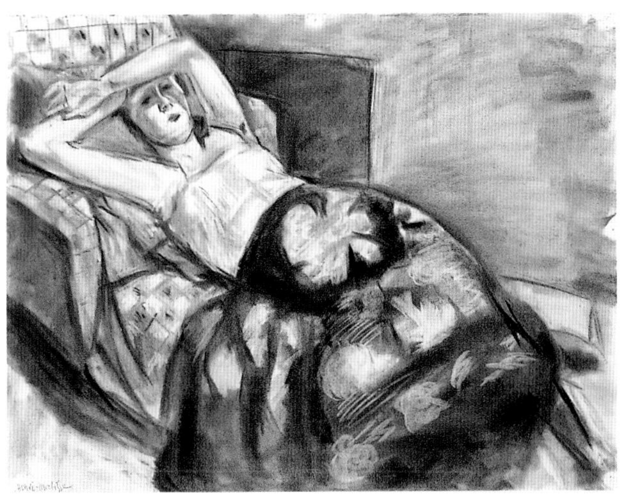

FIG. 6
Henri Matisse, *Reclining Model with a Flowered Robe*, ca. 1923–24. Black chalk with stumping and erasing, 18 7/8 x 24 3/4 in. The Baltimore Museum of Art; The Cone Collection (BMA 1950.12.52). © 2008 Succession H. Matisse/ Artists Rights Society (ARS), New York

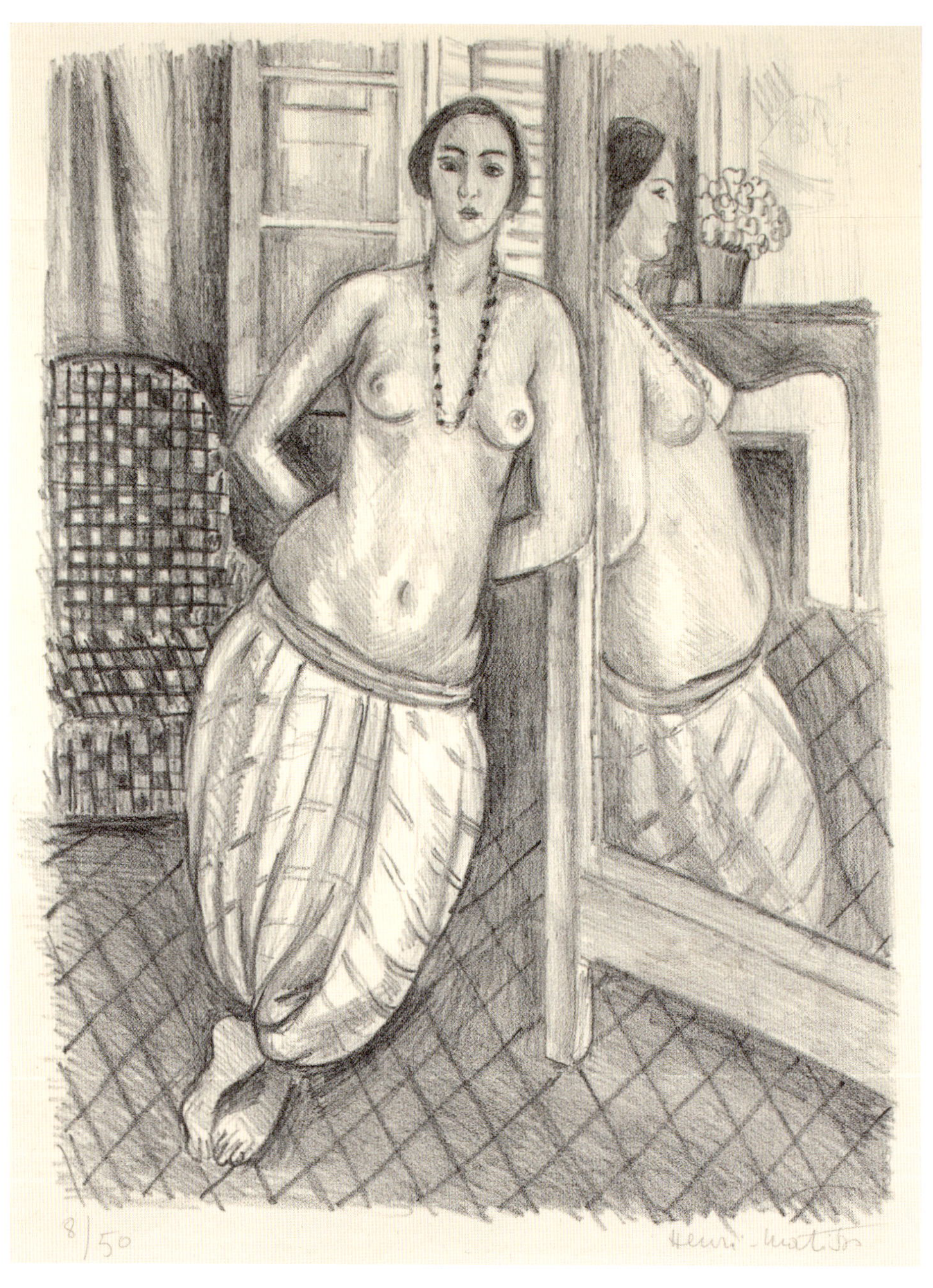

Odalisque in Striped Culottes Reflected in the Mirror, 1923 (cat. no. 19)

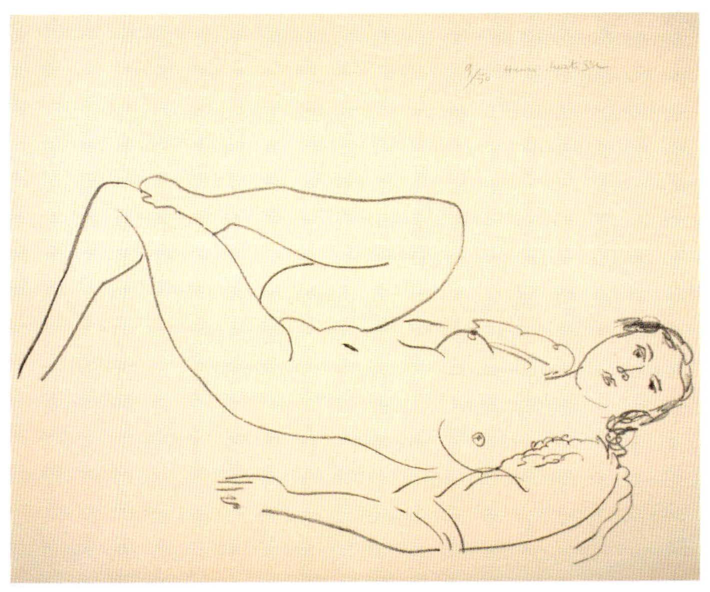

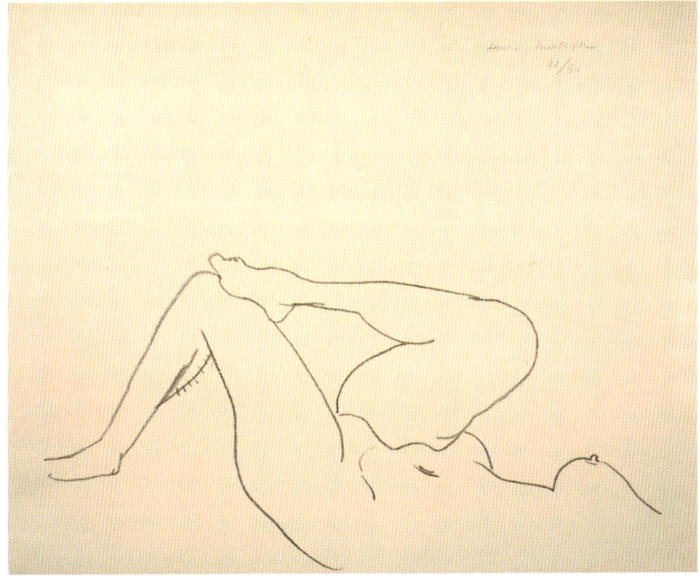

The Turkish Blouse — Study of Legs, 1925 (cat. no. 24)

Study of Legs, 1925 (cat. no. 25)

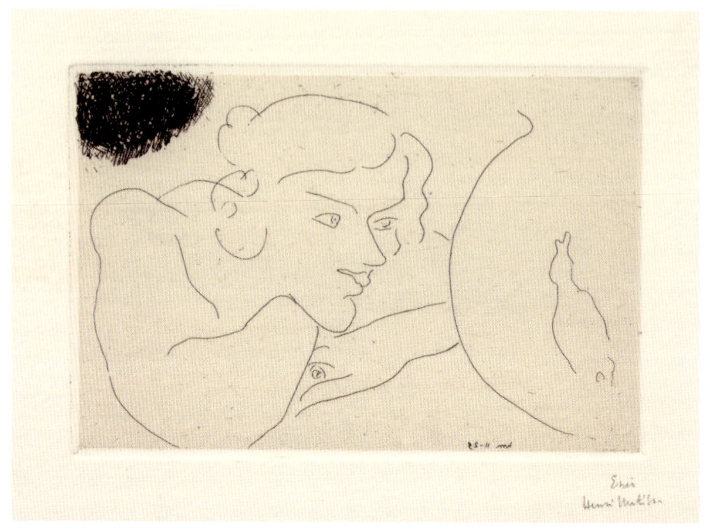

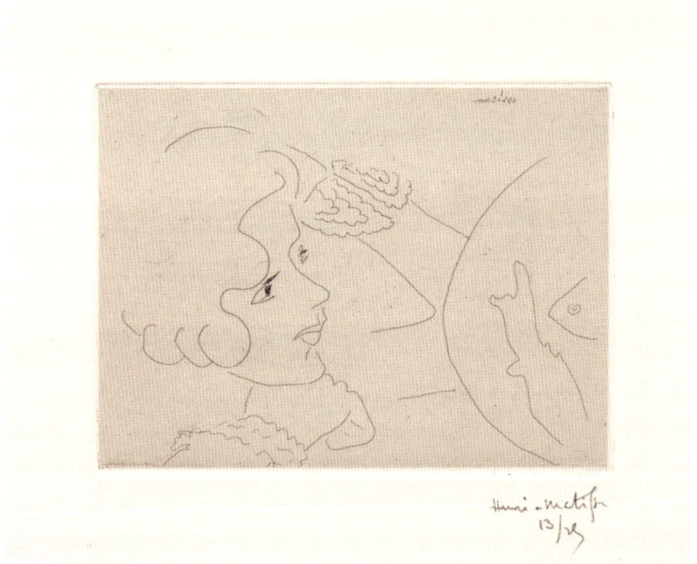

Young Woman Observing the Movements of a Fish, 1929 (cat. no. 32)

Young Woman with Black Eyes Staring at Aquarium, 1929 (cat. no. 36)

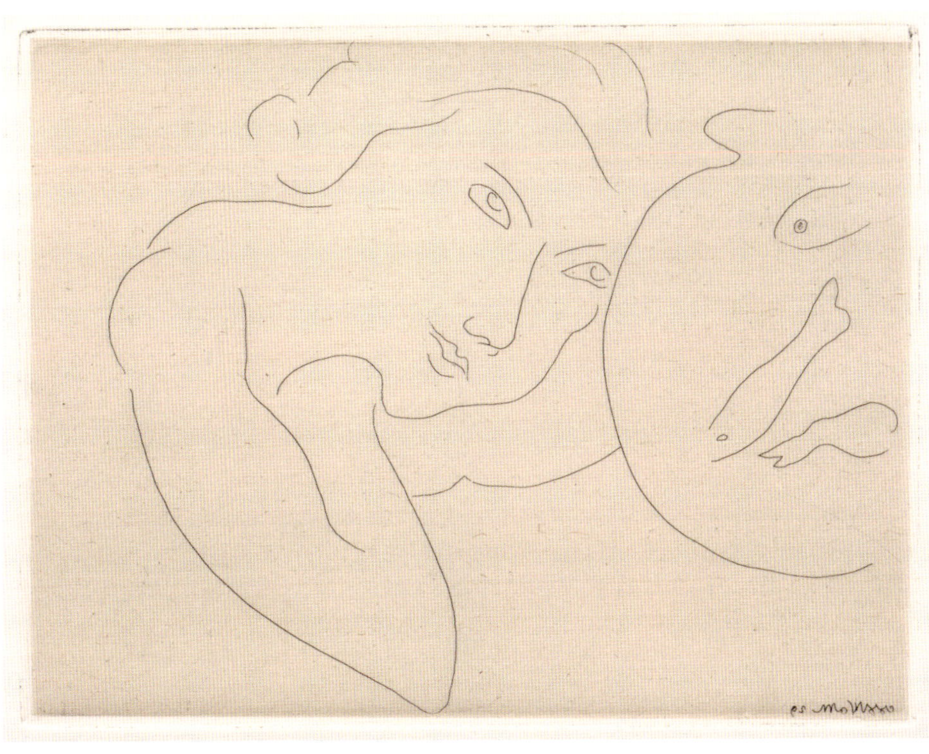

Inclined Head and Fishbowl, 1929 (cat. no. 34)

he published no less than 247 images (108 lithographs and 139 etchings, most of the latter dating from 1929). Such an impressive production implies he had found a market for his prints. The lithographs (many, such as *Model Resting,* drawn directly on the stone but others made using transfer paper) demonstrate a new mode of drawing using shading and modeling, in a manner following the charcoal drawings he was also making in these years (see fig. 6). Such subtle manipulation of chiaroscuro effects required direct work on the stone, with the frequent use of scraping and rubbing to introduce highlights. We now see another self-portrait, this time from 1923, at the age of forty-five, drawn with uncommon intensity directly on the stone with a soft lithographic crayon (cat. no. 17). The blackness of the background, built up with repeated crossing strokes, brings intensity to this severe self-portrait. Without a loss in the spontaneity and individuality of his style, Matisse's prints of these years display a consummate technical control. Clearly, he was extremely well versed in printmaking by this time, and, often working with his daughter Marguerite, he was reportedly a stern taskmaster for the printers. In every aspect of production—the choice of paper, the colors of the inks, and an exacting proofing regimen—he established standards from which the printers dared not depart.

Matisse's prints of the 1920s are directly associated with his work in painting, sculpture, and drawing. Following the subjects of his painting, the lithographs feature odalisques reclining languorously in interiors rich with layers of decorative pattern. Some, such as *Odalisque in Striped Culottes Reflected in the Mirror* (cat. no. 19), actually duplicate paintings (fig. 7), though in reverse, but direct transcription was not the norm. The prints provide an equivalent vision to the paintings and are perhaps more elemental in revealing a developing idea. During most of the decade, Matisse worked with one model, Henriette Darricarrère, seen in the print *Young Girl Leaning on Her Elbows in Front of Flowered Screen* (cat. no. 18) seated at a table, looking out with a detached gaze, surrounded by a swirl of decorative patterns. Though her face is subtly shaded to suggest its volume, her blouse and the vase of flowers merge with the flat decorative screen behind her, creating a single visual plane. Matisse would push the figure-ground relationship even farther in a transfer lithograph of 1924, *Arabesque* (cat. no. 20), where Henriette, dressed in an elaborately embroidered blouse, would be subsumed in the decorative patterns that surround her if not for the linear drawing of her figural contours. The effect compresses flat pattern and volumetric line in a single plane. Simultaneous with such exquisitely luminous prints as *The Persian* (cat. no. 43), which realizes all the modulated luminosity of a charcoal drawing in work directly on the stone, are even more broadly conceived transfer lithographs that advance the approach of *Arabesque* (cat. nos. 28 and 40–42). Here Matisse utilizes a different method of shading, applying uniform patches of tone, revealing the texture of his drawing paper, over passages of contour drawing. This shading is as broad as the linear drawing of the figure and objects, often being laid on the transfer paper with the side of a lithographic crayon.

Exploring the pose of the seated and the reclining nude, Matisse worked with Henriette in an intense collaboration that produced many charcoal drawings, prints, paintings, and a major sculpture, *Large Seated Nude,* a project lasting from 1922 to 1929. In three ambitiously large-scale prints, *Nude on Blue Cushion* (cat. no. 21), *Nude on Blue Cushion next to a Chimney* (cat. no. 22), and *Large Odalisque with Bayadère Culottes* (cat. no. 23), Matisse exploited every effect possible in the medium of lithography, from the deepest black to luminous effects in patterned fabrics and the modeling of flesh. Technically, these prints are more complicated. While they are all transfer lithographs (it is possible to see the watermark of the transfer paper), the

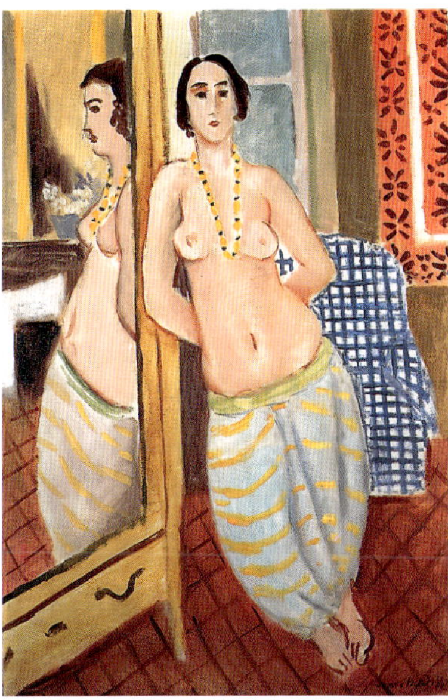

FIG. 7
Henri Matisse, *Standing Odalisque Reflected in a Mirror,* 1923. Oil on canvas, 31 7/8 x 21 3/8 in. The Baltimore Museum of Art; The Cone Collection (BMA 1950.250).

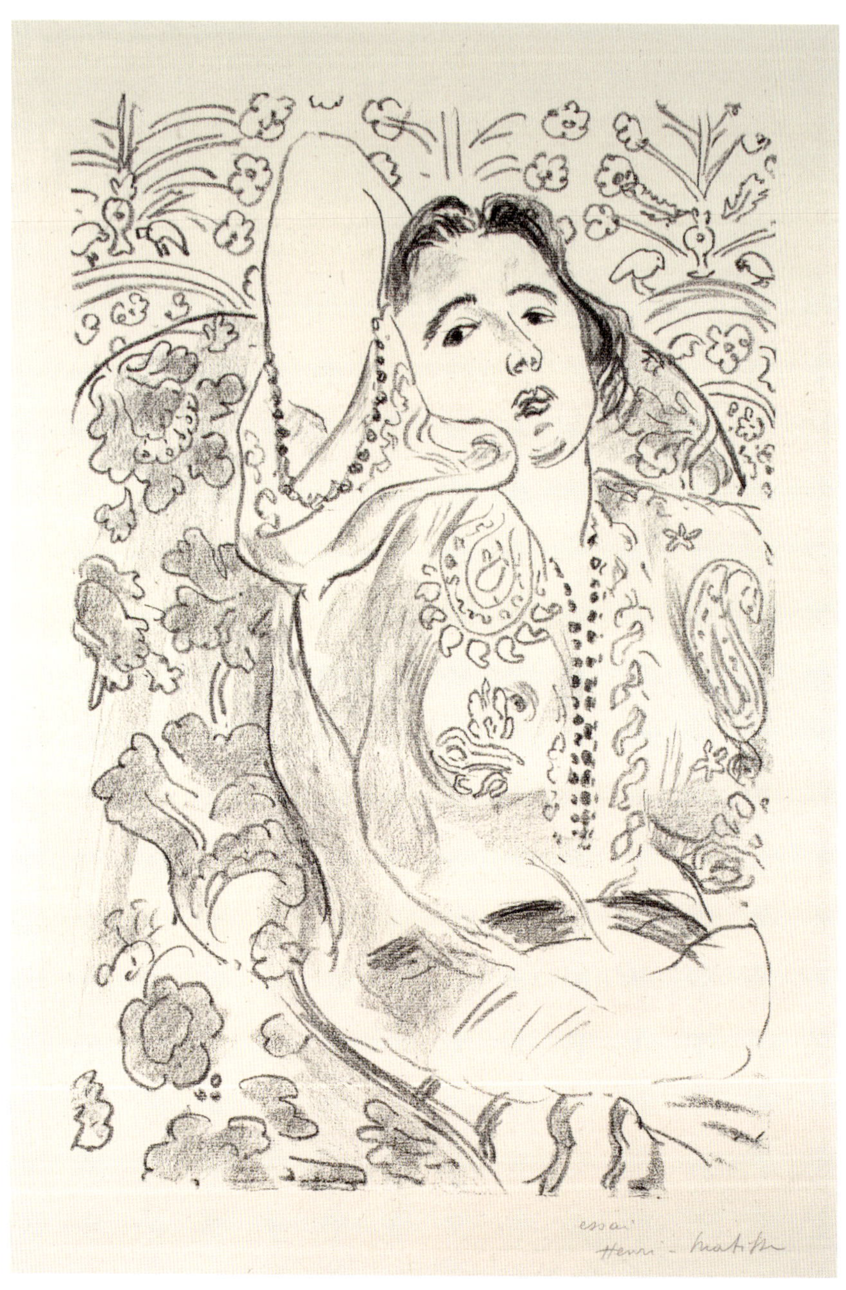

ARABESQUE, 1924 (cat. no. 20)

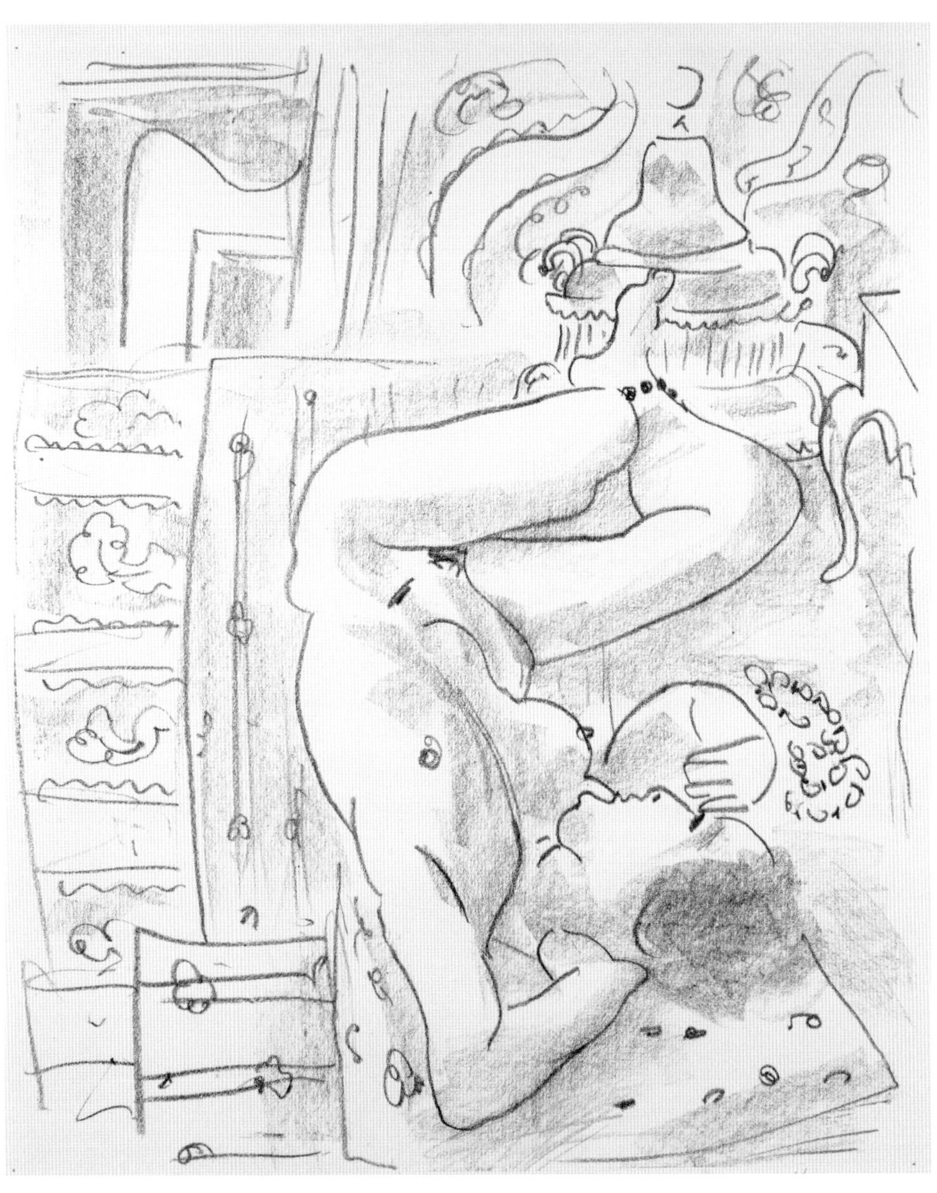

Upside Down Nude with Brazier, 1929 (cat. no. 42)

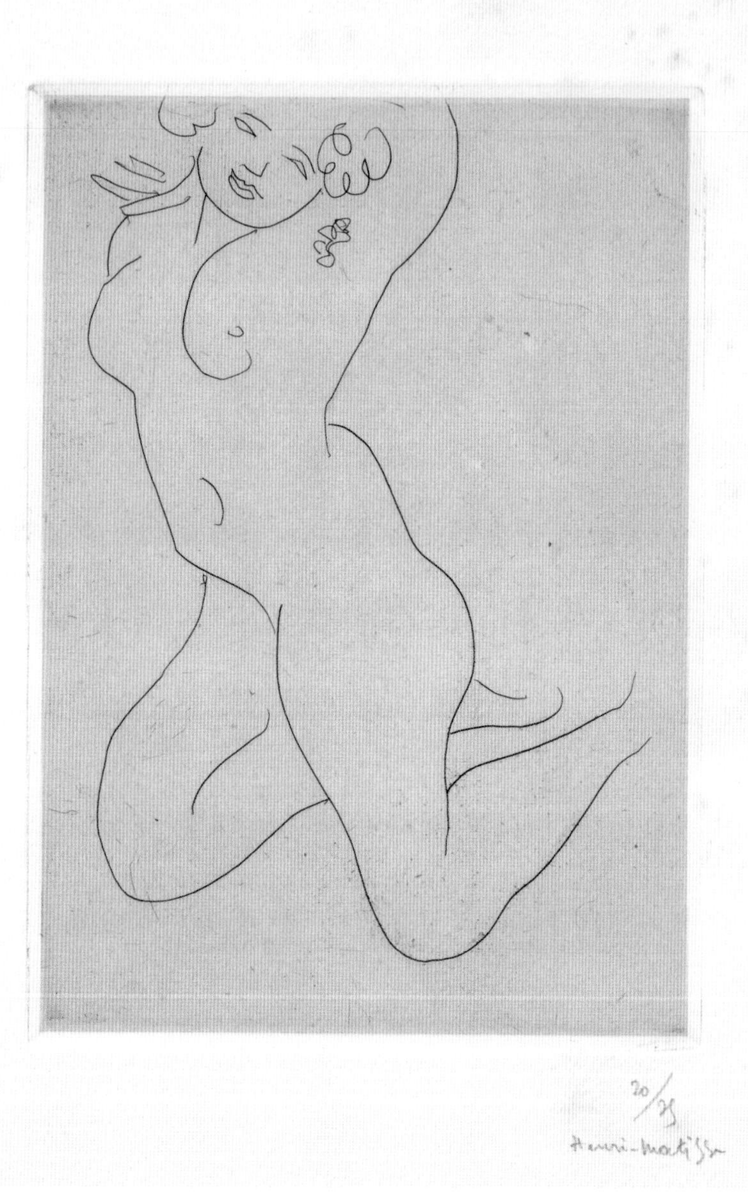

Kneeling Nude, 1930 (cat. no. 45)

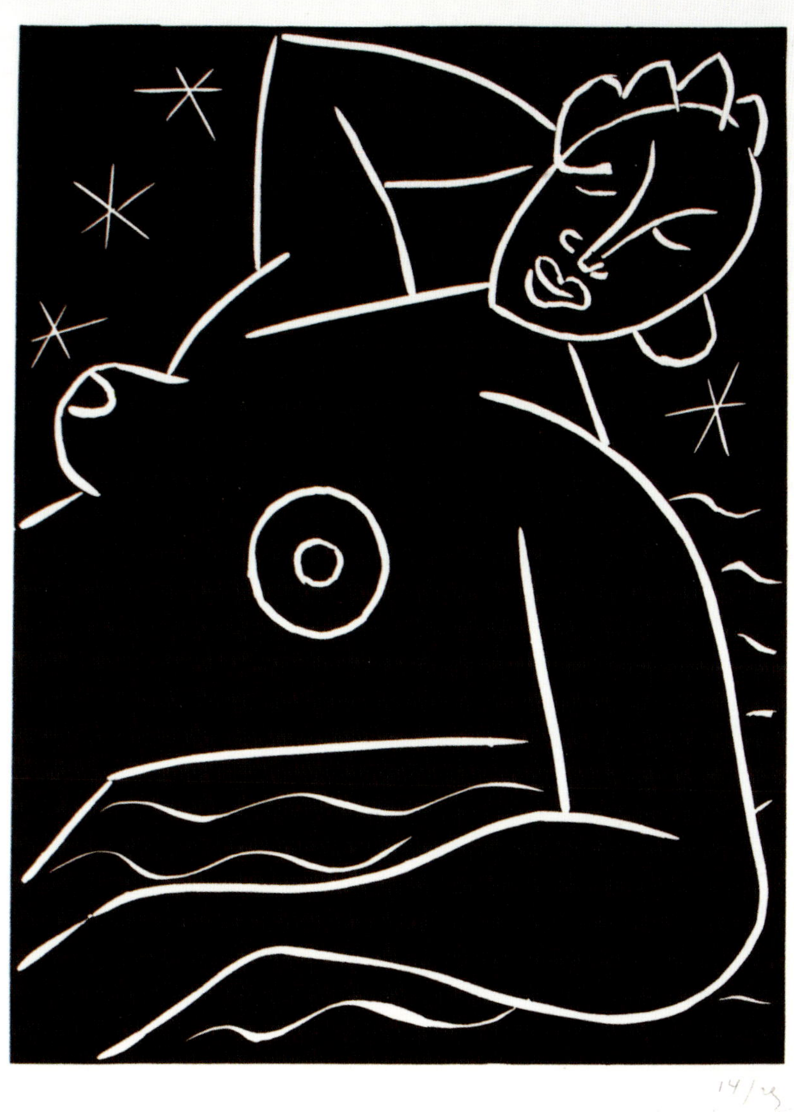

THE FRIGATE, 1938 (cat. no. 49)

prints of nudes on cushions represent two successive stages of the same image where Matisse went back and reworked a drawing already transferred, adding surrounding details such as the chimney. A drawing transferred is not destroyed in the process, though this author has not discovered any drawings actually used for transfer. A photograph of the artist at work in his Nice studio shows many of the reclining-nude prints of these years pinned to the walls, along with other visual references he kept close at hand while working on the sculpture (fig. 8). He also returned to line drawing during these years, as in the transfer lithographs of 1925 that he derived from a playful series of studies in which he worked the model through a number of variations on the reclining pose with legs crossed (cat. nos. 24–26). In 1929, when he was painting less and less often, he made more than a hundred etchings and drypoints. In these, while he remained fascinated with the volumetric description of the figure surrounded by objects and patterns, there is no shading (see cat. no. 37). Groups of these etchings, such as ten small prints of girls watching a bowl of fish (see cat. nos. 31–36), come together as series. The faces and arms of the girls are pressed close to the bowls, and the shorthand reductive drawing joins together observation of both them and the fish.

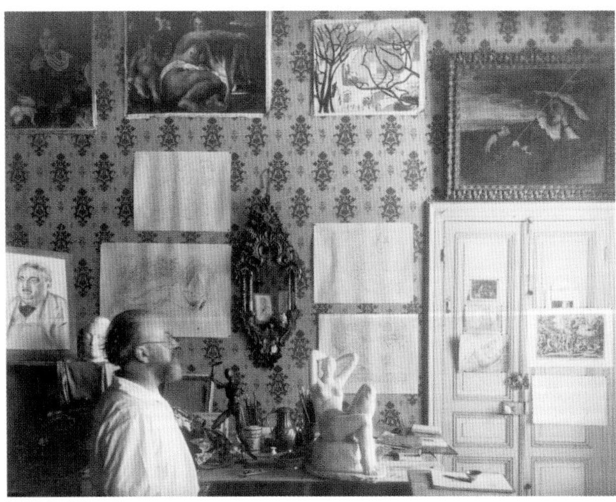

FIG. 8
Henri Matisse at his apartment, no. 1, place Charles-Félix, Nice, France, spring 1926, with plaster cast of early version of *Large Seated Nude* of 1925–29. The Museum of Modern Art, New York. Digital Image © The Museum of Modern Art/Licensed by SCALA/Art Resource, NY

These small prints seem whimsical but speak of the artist's intense concentration on capturing the sensations of the moment.

Matisse would never again be as prolific a maker of individual prints as he was at the end of the 1920s. In the last two decades of his life, his concentration in printmaking was directed primarily to the production of deluxe illustrated books. Although these books are beyond the scope of this exhibition, Lieberman's essay provides an important perspective on the achievement that they represent. Suffice it to say that Matisse pursued bookmaking with the same concentration he applied to all of his creative projects, participating in the design and all other aspects of production. Except for the monotype, the books span all the print techniques he had used thus far and also utilized techniques new to him, such as linocut, aquatint, and, in collaboration with master printers, stencils for the *pochoir* prints derived from his cut-paper designs for *Jazz*. He also produced two color prints. The first, a collaboration with the printer Lacourière (Matisse drew the etched lines, and the printer added the aquatint fields of color), reproduced the first (mismeasured) version of *The Dance* mural of 1932, made for the Barnes Foundation in Merion, Pennsylvania (cat. no. 46); the second, *Marie-José in a Yellow Dress (III)* (cat. no. 61), was one of the last prints he made. Ultimately, however, color in Matisse's prints was superfluous.

The production of single prints closely paralleled Matisse's work on the book projects, demonstrating his commitment to innovation and exploration. In 1938, he took up a new medium, the linoleum cut, a technique in which he could draw a white line against a field of black, as in his earlier monotypes, but this time could print in editions. His consummate control of the medium is well demonstrated in the two-color print *The Siesta* (cat. no. 50), but Matisse's strong commitment to the possibilities of the linoleum-cut medium is most fully realized in the illustrated book *Pasiphaé* (begun in 1943 but not published until 1944).[21] In 1936, he made his first aquatints, which look at first like the monotypes: a stop-out varnish to the plate was used to preserve Matisse's drawn white lines, after which the plate was covered with a uniform aquatint ground to create a field of black. But Matisse made only five works of this kind before reversing the process, using a lift-ground to bare the plate where he had applied a brush to it. The aquatint grain could then be introduced to roughen the plate and hold the ink, creating boldly brushed black lines against fields of unprinted white paper. Matisse wrote, "Black brush drawings contain, in small, the same elements as coloured paintings … that is to say, differentiations in the quality of the surfaces unified by light."[22] If it were not for the texture of the printed aquatint grain, these prints could be facsimiles of the drawings he made in his Vence studio with a large brush and India ink, drawings that represented an alternative mode of working to the gouache-colored cut-paper collages that also engaged him in his later years. The goal of multiplying these new drawings as prints was the impetus for the last flowering of Matisse's creative engagement with printmaking (see fig. 9).

For Matisse, printmaking was an able servant in the realization of his evolving visual ideas. Working sometimes alone and more often with printers, the artist adapted printmaking techniques to his own purposes. Besides turning drawings into multiples, prints offered intrinsic challenges that advanced new ideas and offered fresh possibilities. Prints gave Matisse a way to share with his audience the way he saw, transforming what he observed, synthesizing reality with the process of perception. While his paintings and sculpture appeared in major museums in the United States and abroad, his prints extended the uniqueness of his vision for many collectors' more intimate contemplation.

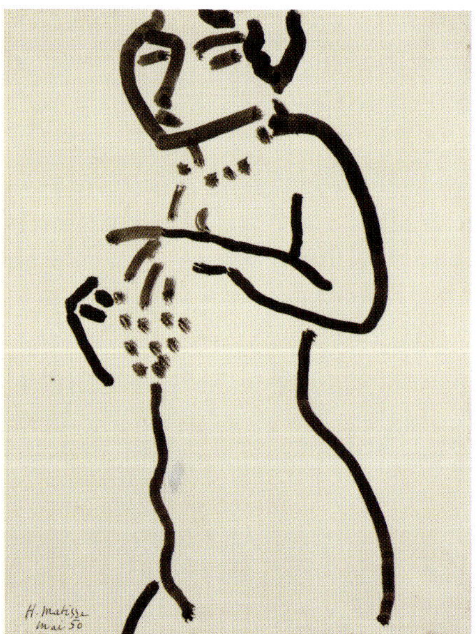

FIG. 9
Henri Matisse, *The Necklace*, 1950. Brush and ink, 20 7/8 x 16 1/8 in. The Museum of Modern Art, New York; The Joan and Lester Avnet Collection (131.1978). © Succession H. Matisse, Paris/ARS, NY. Digital Image © The Museum of Modern Art/Licensed by SCALA/ Art Resource, NY.

Notes to the Text

1 In "How I Made My Books," an essay of 1946 on his illustrated books, Matisse indicates his comprehension of printmaking techniques, particularly his choice of etching for his first book, *Poésies de Stéphane Mallarmé*, published in 1932, and, by contrast, of linoleum cut for a later book, *Pasiphaé*, published in 1944. The essay is reprinted in Jack Flam, ed., *Matisse on Art* (1973, rev. ed. Berkeley: University of California Press, 1995), pp. 166–68. Quotations from it also appear in William S. Lieberman's *Matisse: 50 Years of His Graphic Art* (New York: George Braziller, 1956, pp. 21–22, 24–26); Lieberman's essay in that book is reprinted in the present volume, to which, when Lieberman is cited in these notes, the page numbers refer.

2 See, e.g., Flam, ed., *Matisse on Art*, pp. 46–49, 102–04, 130–32.

3 John O'Brian's *Ruthless Hedonism: The American Reception of Matisse* (Chicago: at the University Press, 1999) focuses on Matisse's American patronage and his relationship to collectors such as Claribel and Etta Cone, among others.

4 See Marguerite Duthuit and Claude Duthuit, *Henri Matisse. Catalogue raisonné de l'oeuvre gravé, 2 vols.* (Paris: l'Imprimerie Union à Paris, 1983), and Claude Duthuit, *Henri Matisse. Catalogue raisonné des ouvrages illustrés* (Paris: l'Imprimerie Union à Paris, 1988), for the editions of Matisse's prints and their sizes and for the number of prints in each book and the size of each book's edition.

5 Picasso's prints total more than 2,000 images and Miro's more than 2,300.

6 Lieberman, "Matisse: 50 Years of His Graphic Art," p. 16.

7 Susan Lambert, *Matisse Lithographs* (London: Victoria and Albert Museum, London, 1972), p. 25 and checklist, pp. 26–75. Lambert undertook a careful study of the lithographs—with particular regard to distinctions between his use of transfer lithography and working directly on the stone—and was also attentive in designating the different papers Matisse used for his lithographs. His response to transfer lithography is also perceptively explored by John Neff in "Henri Matisse: Notes on the Early Prints," in Riva Castleman, *Matisse Prints from The Museum of Modern Art* (New York: Museum of Modern Art, 1986), pp. 21–22.

8 Lieberman, "Matisse: 50 Years of His Graphic Art," pp. 17–18.

9 Lambert, *Matisse Lithographs*, pp. 12–13.

10 See Pat Gilmour, "Cher Monsieur Clot ... Auguste Clot and His Role as a Colour Lithographer," in Gilmour, ed., *Lasting Impressions: Lithography as Art* (Philadelphia: University of Pennsylvania Press, 1988), pp. 129–82.

11 John Elderfield, in Magdalena Dabrowski, Elderfield, and John Golding, eds., *The Drawings of Henri Matisse* (New York: The Museum of Modern Art, 1984), p. 41.

12 Lieberman, "Matisse: 50 Years of His Graphic Art," p. 16, note 3, p. 31.

13 See Bernice Rose, *A Century of Modern Drawing from The Museum of Modern Art* (London: British Museum Publications, 1982), p. 17.

14 Elderfield, *The Drawings of Henri Matisse*, p. 41.

15 Lieberman, "Matisse: 50 Years of His Graphic Art," p. 16. See also Jay Fisher, "Drawing Is Sculpture Is Drawing," in Ann Boulton, Fisher, Dorothy Kosinski, et al., *Henri Matisse: Painter as Sculptor* (Baltimore: Baltimore Museum of Art; and Dallas: Dallas Museum of Art and Nasher Sculpture Center, in association with Yale University Press, New Haven, 2007), pp. 35–36.

16 Elderfield, *The Drawings of Henri Matisse*, pp. 40–41.

17 Lieberman, "Matisse: 50 Years of His Graphic Art," p. 16, note 2, p. 31; Elderfield, *The Drawings of Henri Matisse*, pp. 56–57.

18 *Cinquante dessins par Henri Matisse* (Paris: Galerie Bernheim Jeune, 1920), and *Dessins: Thèmes et variations* (Paris: Martin Fabiani, 1943).

19 Claude Duthuit, *Catalogue raisonné des ouvrages illustrés*, pp. 36–42.

20 See Fisher, "Drawing Is Sculpture Is Drawing," p. 45.

21 See Lieberman, "Matisse: 50 Years of His Graphic Art," pp. 24–26, in Flam, *Matisse on Art*, p. 167, Matisse's 1946 article on his books, "How I Made My Books," is reprinted. The long gestation of the *Pasiphaé* book, particularly the exchange of letters between the author, Henri de Montherlant, and Matisse about the use of linoleum cuts, is related in Claude Duthuit, *Catalogue raisonné des ouvrages illustrés*, pp. 437–38.

22 Matisse, quoted in Elderfield, *The Drawings of Henri Matisse*, p. 128.

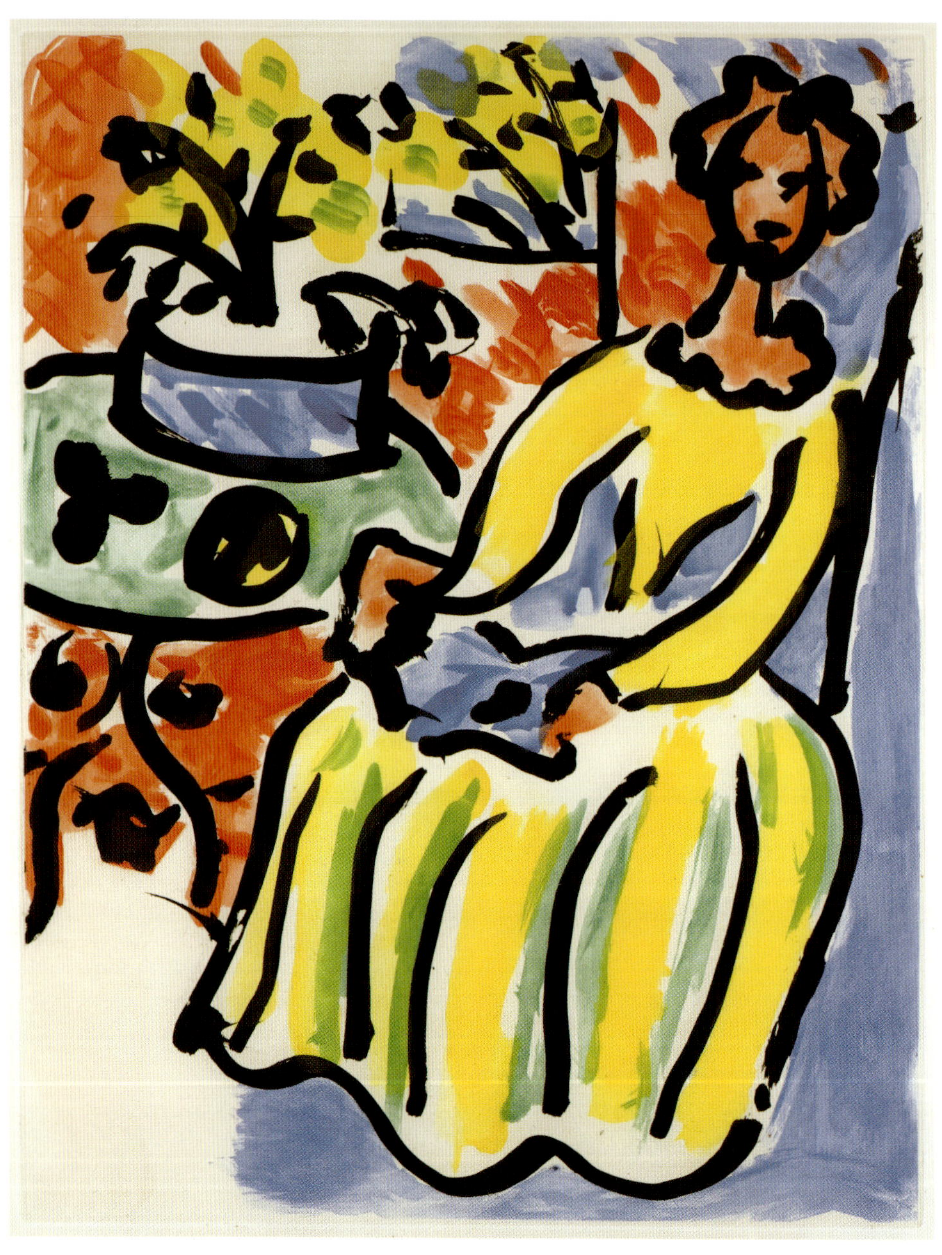

Marie-José in a Yellow Dress (III), 1950 (cat. no. 61)

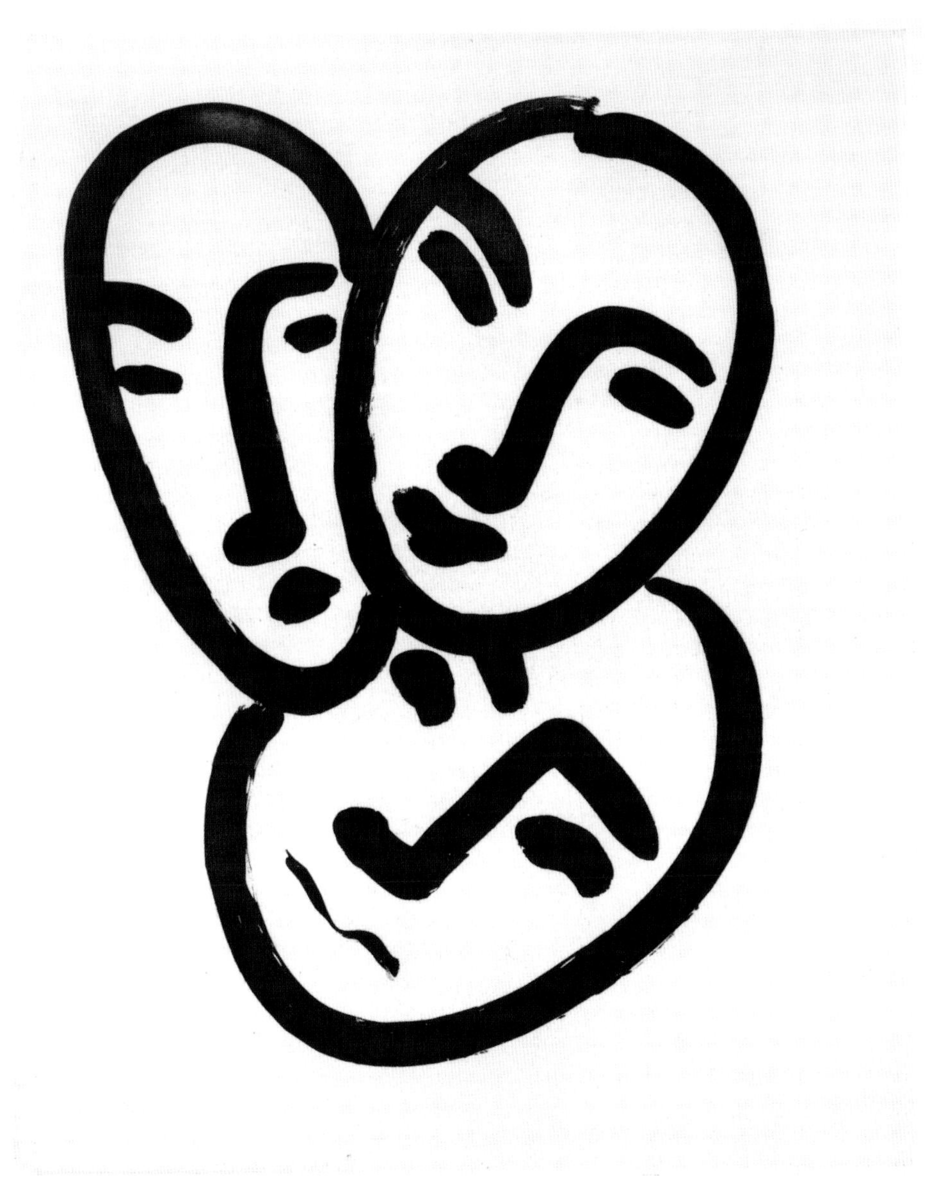

Three Heads. To Friendship (Apollinaire), 1951–52 (cat. no. 63)

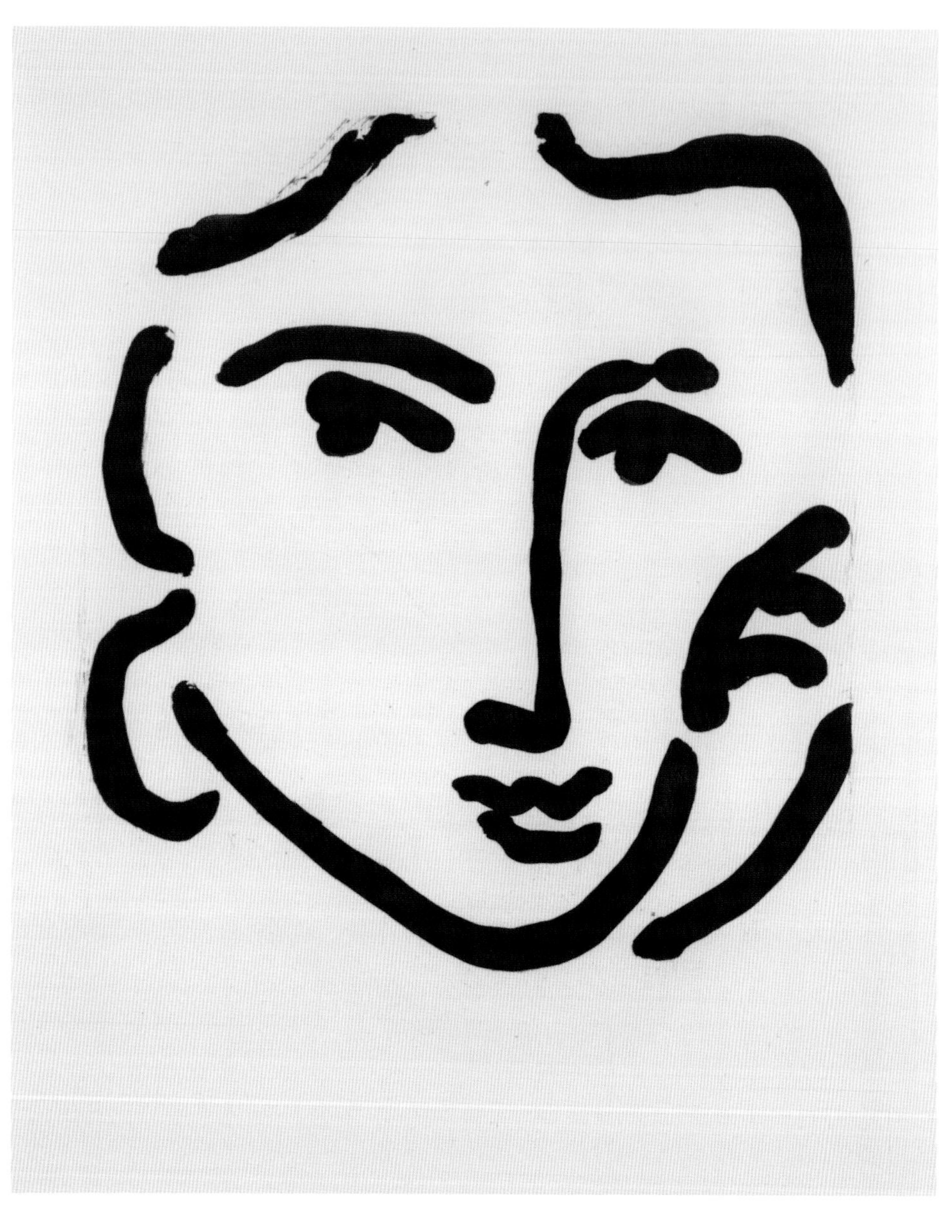

Nadia with a Serious Expression, 1948 (cat. no. 55)

ILLUSTRATED CHECKLIST

The description of medium represents recent examination by the author and Thomas Primeau, Director of Conservation and Paper Conservator, The Baltimore Museum of Art.

The notation *Duthuit* followed by a number designates the number attached to given prints by the catalogue raisonné of Matisse's print oeuvre. Written by Marguerite Duthuit and Claude Duthuit, these volumes are cited in the bibliography for this publication. Because of the descriptive nature of the titles for Matisse prints and the similarity of subjects, use of the catalogue raisonné number is essential to identifying specific Matisse prints. Dates and titles are consistent with those cited in the catalogue raisonné.

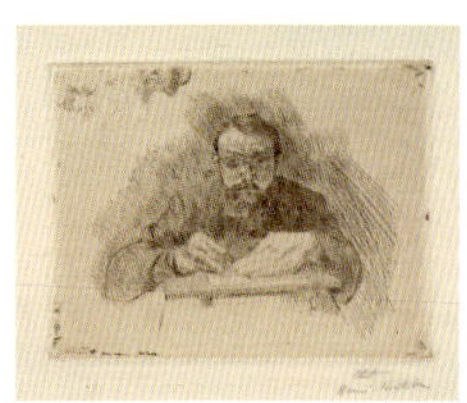

1. Henri Matisse Engraving
1900–03. Drypoint
Image: 5 7/8 x 7 7/8 inches (14.9 x 20 cm)
Sheet: 9 13/16 x 12 15/16 in. (25 x 33 cm)
Pierre and Tana Matisse Foundation (1303 - 105083)
Duthuit 1
(p. 34)

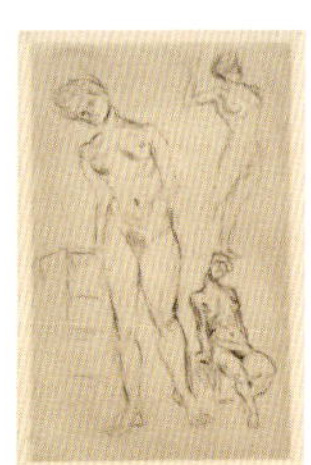

2. Three Nudes, One Leaning on a Stool
1900–03. Drypoint
Image: 5 7/8 x 3 15/16 in. (14.9 x 10 cm)
Sheet: 10 13/16 x 7 1/16 in. (27.5 x 18 cm)
Pierre and Tana Matisse Foundation (1586 - 105089)
Duthuit 3

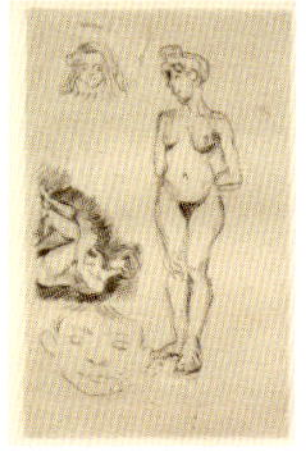

3. Two Nudes, Two Children's Heads
1900–03. Drypoint
Image: 5 7/8 x 3 15/16 in. (15 x 10 cm)
Sheet: 13 x 10 in. (33 x 25.5 cm)
Pierre and Tana Matisse Foundation (1583 - 105086)
Duthuit 6

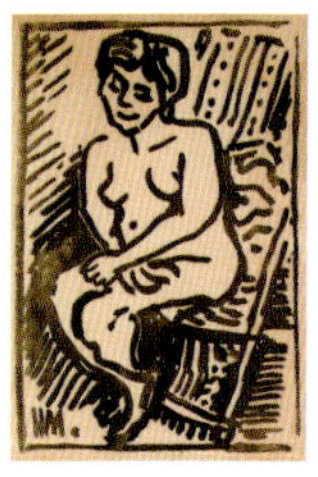

4. Small Black Woodcut
1906. Woodcut
Image: 12 1/4 x 8 3/8 in. (31.1 x 21.2 cm)
Sheet: 18 1/8 x 11 1/4 in. (46 x 28.5 cm)
Pierre and Tana Matisse Foundation (1711 - 108012)
Duthuit 319

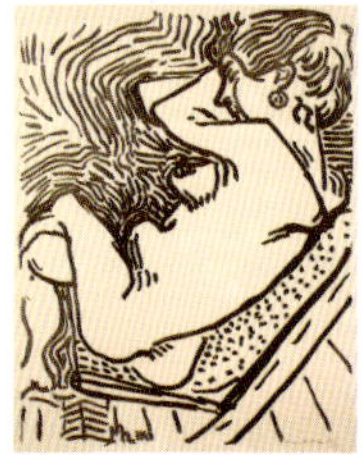

5. The Large Woodcut
1906. Woodcut
Image: 18 11/16 x 14 15/16 in. (47.5 x 38 cm)
Sheet: 22 5/8 x 18 1/8 in. (57.5 x 46 cm)
Pierre and Tana Matisse Foundation (1733 - 110001)
Duthuit 317
(p. 42)

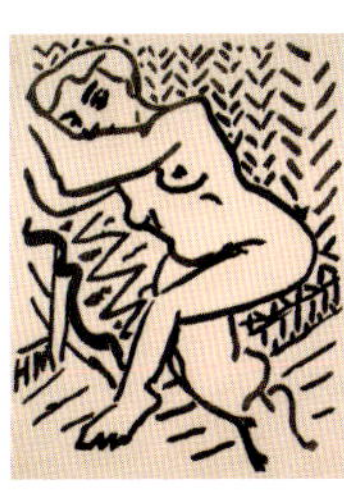

6. Small Light Woodcut
1906. Woodcut
Image: 13 7/16 x 10 1/2 in. (34.2 x 26.6 cm)
Sheet: 18 1/8 x 11 1/4 in. (46 x 28.5 cm)
Pierre and Tana Matisse Foundation (1482 - 101001)
Duthuit 318

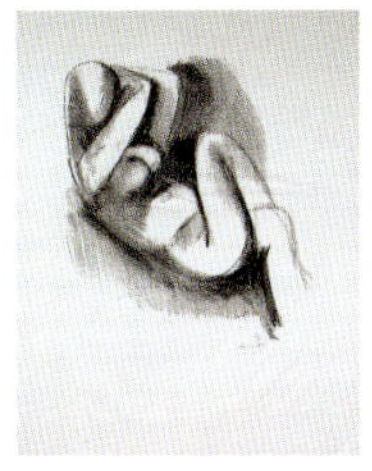

7. The Large Nude
1906. Crayon, brush and tusche lithograph with scraping
Image: 11 1/4 x 9 15/16 in. (28.5 x 25.3 cm)
Sheet: 17 3/4 x 13 15/16 in. (45 x 35.3 cm)
Pierre and Tana Matisse Foundation (1714 - 109001)
Duthuit 403
(p. 48)

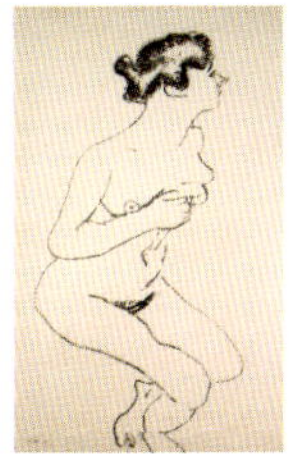

8. Crouching Nude with Black Hair, in Profile
1906. Crayon transfer lithograph
Image: 14 3/4 x 10 5/8 in. (37.4 x 27 cm)
Sheet: 17 3/4 x 11 in. (45 x 28 cm)
Pierre and Tana Matisse Foundation (1483 - 101002)
Duthuit 395
(p. 43)

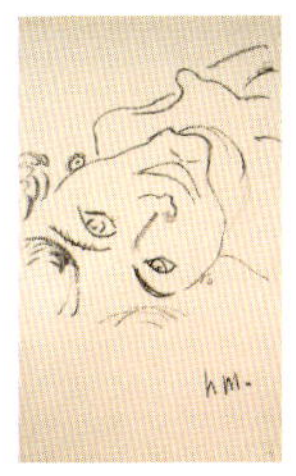

9. Head Turned Upside Down
1906. Crayon transfer lithograph
Image: 11 x 10 13/16 in. (28 x 27.5 cm)
Sheet: 17 5/8 x 10 15/16 in. (44.9 x 27.8 cm)
Pierre and Tana Matisse Foundation (1485 - 101005)
Duthuit 397

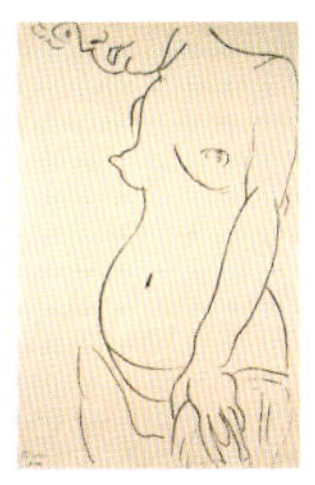

10. Three-quarter View of Nude with Cropped Head
1913. Crayon transfer lithograph
Image and sheet: 20 3/16 x 11 15/16 in. (51.2 x 30.3 cm)
Pierre and Tana Matisse Foundation (1487 - 101007)
Duthuit 409

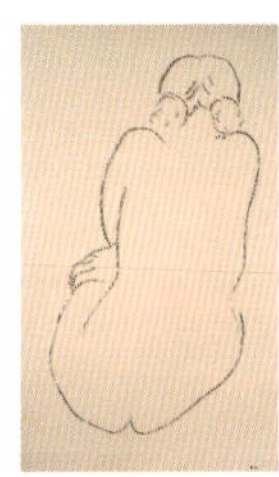

11. SEATED NUDE, VIEWED FROM BEHIND

1913. Crayon transfer lithograph
Image: 16 5/8 x 9 1/2 in. (42.2 x 24.2 cm)
Sheet: 19 3/5 x 13 in. (50.3 x 33 cm)
Pierre and Tana Matisse Foundation (1491 - 101011)
Duthuit 412
(p. 49)

12. OLIVARÈS

1914. Etching
Image: 6 5/16 x 2 3/8 in. (16.1 x 6.1 cm)
Sheet: 10 15/16 x 7 3/8 in. (27.7 x 18.8 cm)
Pierre and Tana Matisse Foundation (1574 - 105073)
Duthuit 41

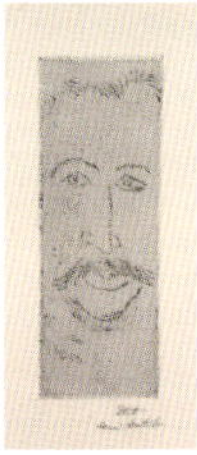

13. PORTRAIT OF WALTER PACH

1914. Etching
Image: 6 5/16 x 2 3/8 in. (16.1 x 6 cm)
Sheet: 11 x 7 5/16 in. (28 x 18.7 cm)
Pierre and Tana Matisse Foundation (1573 - 105072)
Duthuit 42
(p. 38)

14. CROPPED NUDE II

1914. Monotype
Image: 6 5/16 x 2 3/8 in. (16 x 6 cm)
Sheet: 13 3/4 x 11 in. (35 x 28 cm)
Pierre and Tana Matisse Foundation (1706 - 108002)
Duthuit 325
(p. 8)

15. THE PAINTER ALBERT MARQUET

1914–15. Monotype
Image: 5 11/16 x 4 1/8 in. (14.5 x 10.5 cm)
Sheet: 12 13/16 x 9 7/8 in. (32.5 x 25 cm)
Pierre and Tana Matisse Foundation (1708 - 108007)
Duthuit 329
(p. 39)

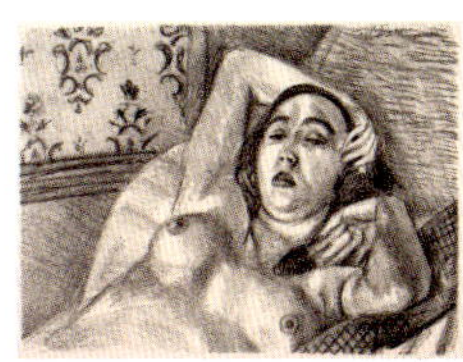

16. Model Resting
1922. Crayon lithograph with scraping
Image and sheet: 8 ¾ x 11 15/16 in. (22.2 x 30.4 cm)
Pierre and Tana Matisse Foundation (1499 - 101047)
Duthuit 416

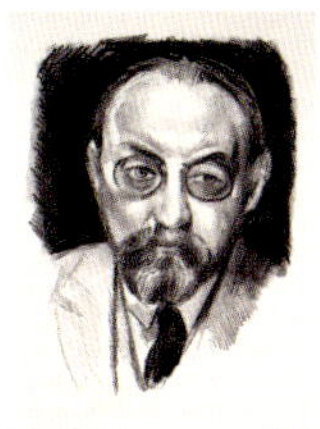

17. Self-portrait
1923. Crayon lithograph
Image: 12 13/16 x 10 1/16 in. (32.5 x 25.5 cm)
Sheet: 20 ½ x 15 5/16 in. (52 x 39 cm)
Pierre and Tana Matisse Foundation (1736 - 110007)
Duthuit 440

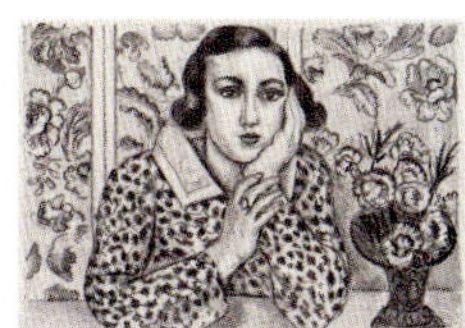

18. Young Girl Leaning on Her Elbows in front of Flowered Screen
1923. Crayon lithograph with scraping
Image: 7 3/16 x 10 5/16 in. (18.3 x 26.2 cm)
Sheet: 11 3/8 x 14 ¼ in. (29 x 36.2 cm)
Pierre and Tana Matisse Foundation (1732 - 109020)
Duthuit 439

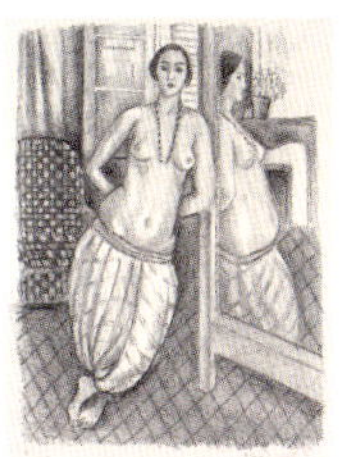

19. Odalisque in Striped Culottes Reflected in the Mirror
1923. Crayon lithograph with scraping
Image: 15 ¾ x 11 13/16 in. (40 x 30 cm)
Sheet: 24 13/16 x 18 13/16 in. (63 x 47.8 cm)
Pierre and Tana Matisse Foundation (1720 - 109007)
Duthuit 433
(p. 54)

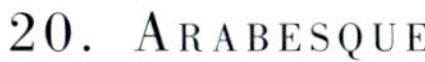

20. Arabesque
1924. Crayon transfer lithograph
Image: 19 x 12 5/8 in. (48.3 x 32 cm)
Sheet: 24 ½ x 18 1/8 in. (62.2 x 46 cm)
Pierre and Tana Matisse Foundation (1728 - 109016)
Duthuit 449
(p. 60)

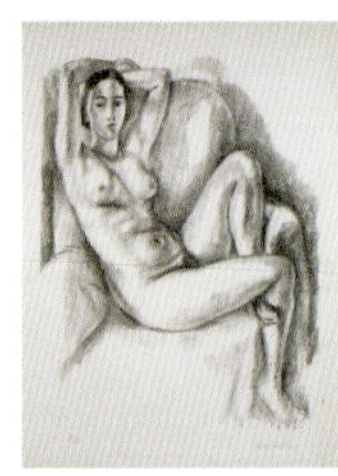

21. Nude on Blue Cushion
1924. Crayon transfer lithograph
Image: 24 3/16 x 18 11/16 in. (61.5 x 47.5 cm)
Sheet: 29 1/2 x 22 in. (75 x 56 cm)
Pierre and Tana Matisse Foundation (1503 - 101051)
Duthuit 442

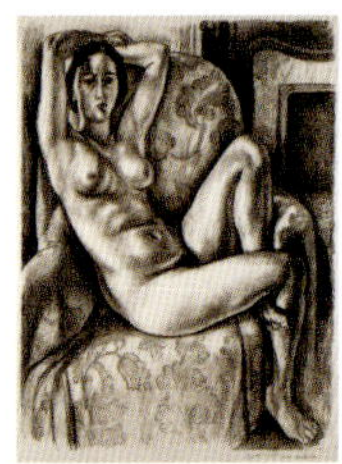

22. Nude on Blue Cushion Next to a Chimney
1925. Crayon transfer lithograph (after rework of drawing used for transfer for *Nude on Blue Cushion*, cat. no. 21)
Image: 25 1/16 x 18 13/16 in. (63.6 x 47.8 cm)
Sheet: 29 3/4 x 22 in. (75.5 x 56 cm)
Pierre and Tana Matisse Foundation (1265 - 101056)
Duthuit 454

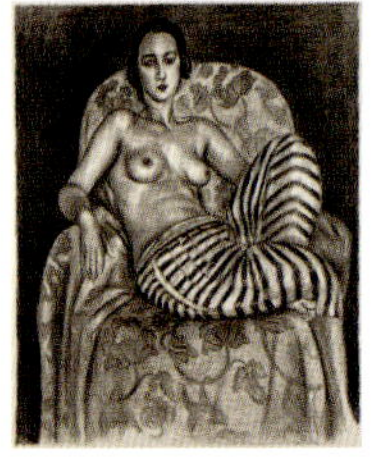

23. Large Odalisque with Bayadère Culottes
1925. Crayon transfer lithograph with scraping
Image: 21 5/16 x 17 3/8 in. (54.2 x 44.2 cm)
Sheet: 29 1/2 x 22 1/16 in. (75 x 56 cm)
Pierre and Tana Matisse Foundation (1727 - 109014)
Duthuit 455
(p. 50)

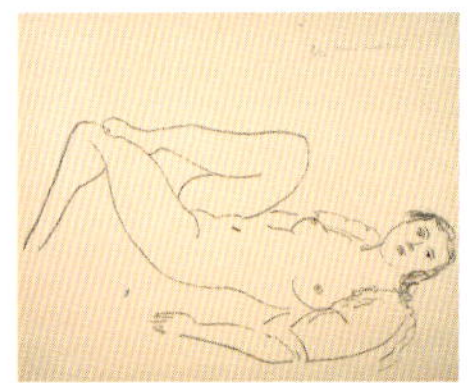

24. The Turkish Blouse — Study of Legs
1925. Crayon transfer lithograph
Image: 11 13/16 x 21 5/16 in. (30 x 54.2 cm)
Sheet: 17 15/16 x 22 1/16 in. (45.5 x 56 cm)
Pierre and Tana Matisse Foundation (1279 - 101070)
Duthuit 459
(p. 55)

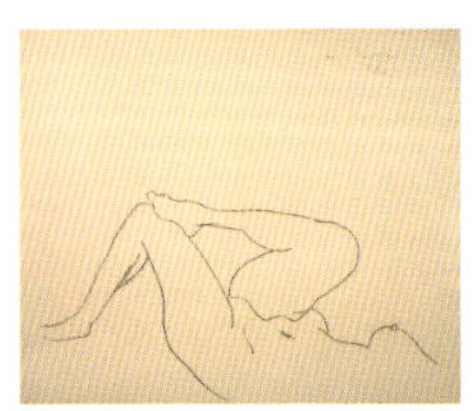

25. Study of Legs
1925. Crayon transfer lithograph
Image: 9 13/16 x 19 11/16 in. (25 x 50 cm)
Sheet: 17 15/16 x 22 1/6 in. (45.5 x 56 cm)
Pierre and Tana Matisse Foundation (1272 - 101063)
Duthuit 460
(p. 55)

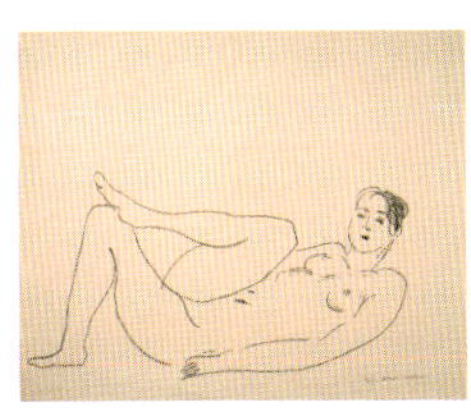

26. Reclining Nude, Leg Folded Up — Study of Legs
1925. Crayon transfer lithograph
Image: 10 x 18 11/16 in. (25.4 x 47.5 cm)
Sheet: 18 x 22 1/16 in. (45.7 x 56 cm)
Pierre and Tana Matisse Foundation (1276 - 101067)
Duthuit 461

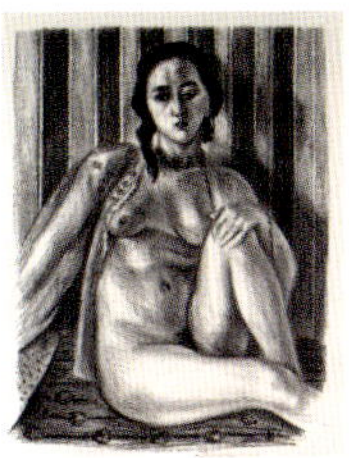

27. Seated Nude with Tulle Shirt
1925. Crayon lithograph with scraping
Image: 14 1/2 x 11 in. (36.8 x 27.9 cm)
Sheet: 21 5/8 x 14 5/8 in. (55 x 37.2 cm)
Pierre and Tana Matisse Foundation (2170 - M074)
Duthuit 465
(p. 14)

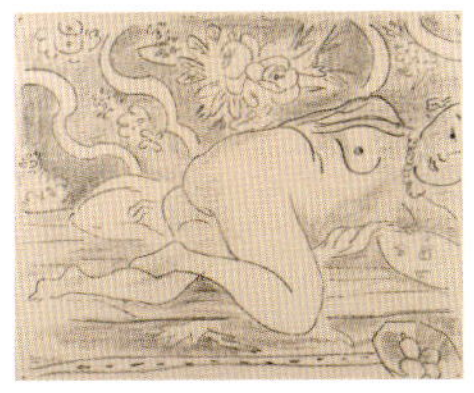

28. Reclining Nude with Bowl of Fruit
1926. Crayon transfer lithograph
Image: 17 1/4 x 21 3/8 in. (43.8 x 54.3 cm)
Sheet: 18 1/8 x 22 1/16 in. (46 x 56 cm)
Pierre and Tana Matisse Foundation (1284 - 101075)
Duthuit 475

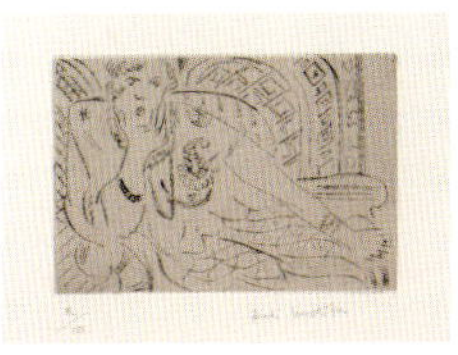

29. Young Woman in front of a Mashrabiya Background
1926. Drypoint
Image: 4 x 5 13/16 in. (10.1 x 14.8 cm)
Sheet: 8 13/16 x 12 1/4 in. (22.5 x 31 cm)
Pierre and Tana Matisse Foundation (1595 - 105098)
Duthuit 99

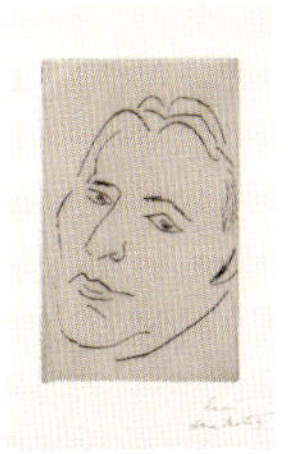

30. The Pianist Alfred Cortot
1927. Drypoint
Image: 5 7/16 x 3 3/8 in. (13.8 x 8.6 cm)
Sheet: 14 15/16 x 11 in. (38 x 28 cm)
Pierre and Tana Matisse Foundation (1535 - 105022)
Duthuit 112

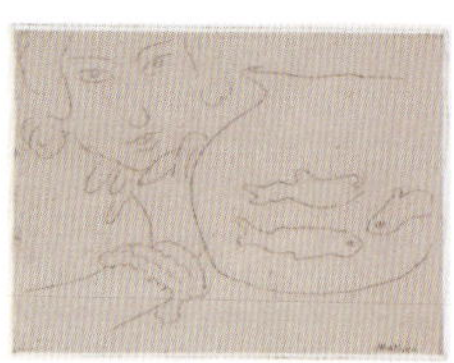

31. Face of Young Woman and Bowl with Three Fish
1929. Etching
Image: 3 5/8 x 4 15/16 in. (9.2 x 12.5 cm)
Sheet: 11 x 14 15/16 in. (28 x 38 cm)
Pierre and Tana Matisse Foundation (1554 - 105046)
Duthuit 169

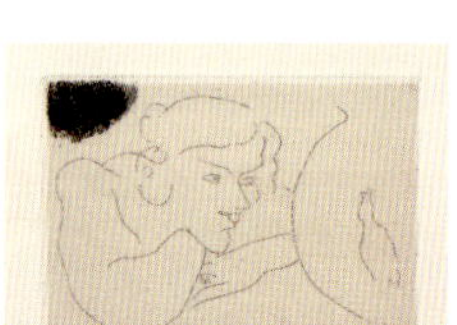

32. Young Woman Observing the Movements of a Fish
1929. Etching
Image: 3 15/16 x 5 15/16 in. (10 x 15.1 cm)
Sheet: 11 x 14 15/16 in. (28 x 38 cm)
Pierre and Tana Matisse Foundation (1562 - 105055)
Duthuit 171
(p. 56)

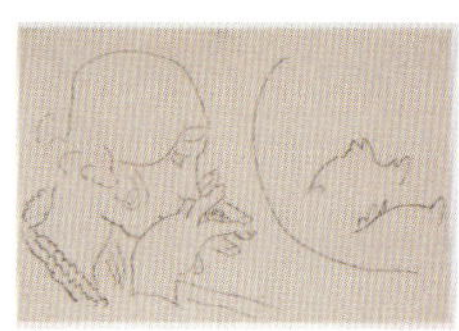

33. Young Woman Looking at a Bowl of Goldfish
1929. Etching
Image: 3 15/16 x 5 15/16 in. (10 x 15.1 cm)
Sheet: 11 1/4 x 14 15/16 in. (28.5 x 38 cm)
Pierre and Tana Matisse Foundation (1600 - 105106)
Duthuit 172

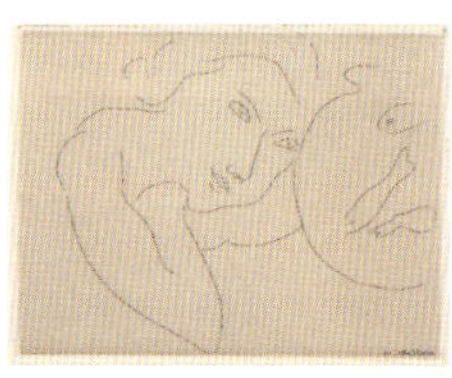

34. Inclined Head and Fishbowl
1929. Etching
Image: 5 7/8 x 7 11/16 in. (14.9 x 19.6 cm)
Sheet: 11 1/4 x 14 15/16 in. (28.5 x 38 cm)
Pierre and Tana Matisse Foundation (1610 - 105117)
Duthuit 177
(p. 57)

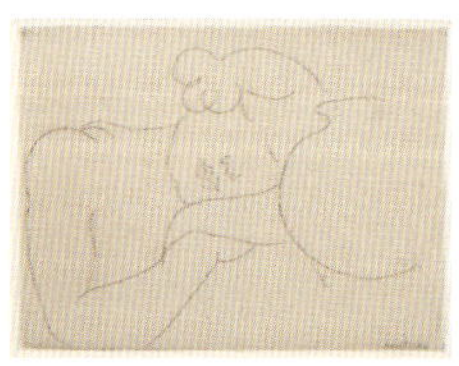

35. Young Woman Sleeping near a Fishbowl
1929. Etching
Image: 4 7/8 x 6 9/16 in. (12.4 x 16.7 cm)
Sheet: 11 x 14 15/16 in. (28 x 38 cm)
Pierre and Tana Matisse Foundation (1659 - 106042)
Duthuit 178

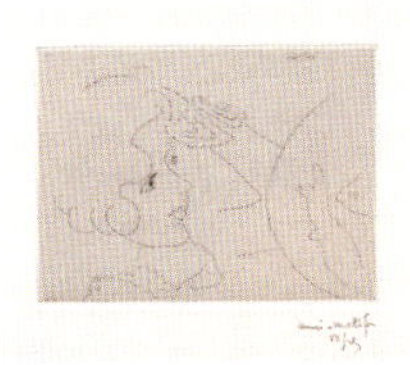

36. Young Woman with Black Eyes Staring at Aquarium
1929. Etching
Image: 3 5/8 x 4 15/16 in. (9.2 x 12.5 cm)
Sheet: 11 x 14 15/16 in. (28 x 38 cm)
Pierre and Tana Matisse Foundation (1616 - 105123)
Duthuit 179
(p. 56)

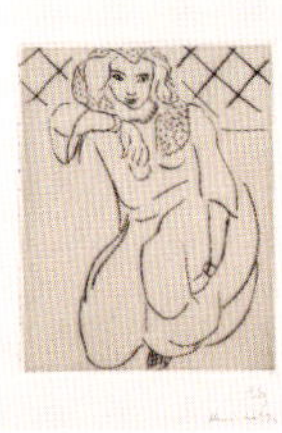

37. Crouching Oriental, Veil on Her Head
1929. Drypoint
Image: 6 1/8 x 4 13/16 in. (15.6 x 12.3 cm)
Sheet: 14 15/16 x 11 1/4 in. (38 x 28.5 cm)
Pierre and Tana Matisse Foundation (1548 - 105039)
Duthuit 155

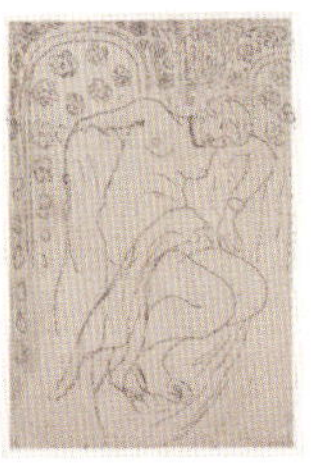

38. Sleeping Figure in front of a Mashrabiya Background
1929. Etching
Image: 9 13/16 x 7 1/16 in. (25 x 17.9 cm)
Sheet: 14 15/16 x 11 in. (38 x 28 cm)
Pierre and Tana Matisse Foundation (1522 - 105007)
Duthuit 127
(p. 51)

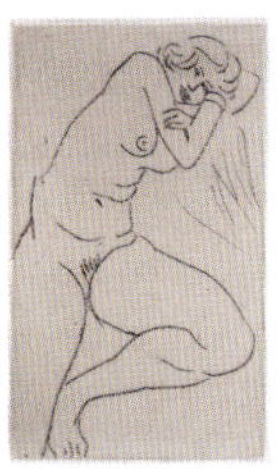

39. Seated Nude, Her Head in Her Arms
1929. Drypoint
Image: 7 15/16 x 4 3/4 in. (20.1 x 12 cm)
Sheet: 14 3/4 x 11 in. (37.5 x 28 cm)
Pierre and Tana Matisse Foundation (1518 - 105003)
Duthuit 117

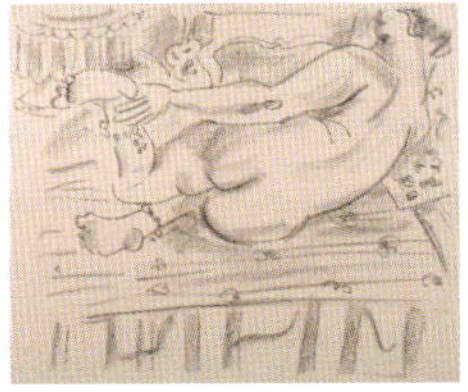

40. Reclining Nude from the Back
1929. Crayon transfer lithograph
Image: 18 1/8 x 22 1/16 in. (46 x 56 cm)
Sheet: 19 7/8 x 25 15/16 in. (50.5 x 66 cm)
Pierre and Tana Matisse Foundation (1258 - 101034)
Duthuit 496

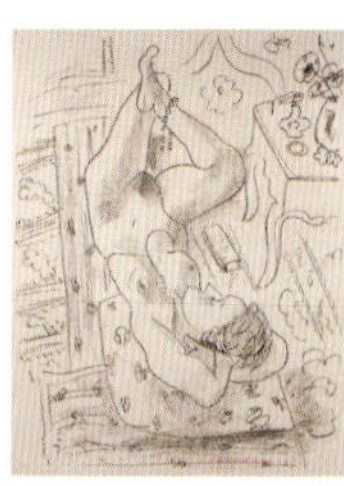

41. Upside Down Nude, near a Louis XV Table

1929. Crayon transfer lithograph
Image: 22 x 18 1/8 in. (55.9 x 46 cm)
Sheet: 26 x 19 11/16 in. (66 x 50 cm)
Pierre and Tana Matisse Foundation (1296 - 102003)
Duthuit 499

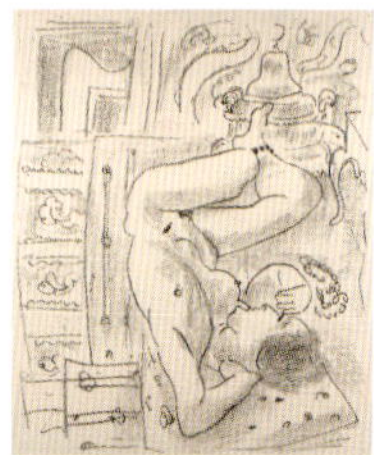

42. Upside Down Nude with Brazier

1929. Crayon transfer lithograph
Image: 21 15/16 x 18 1/8 in. (55.7 x 46 cm)
Sheet: 26 x 19 15/16 in. (66 x 50.5 cm)
Pierre and Tana Matisse Foundation (1299 - 102007)
Duthuit 500
(p. 61)

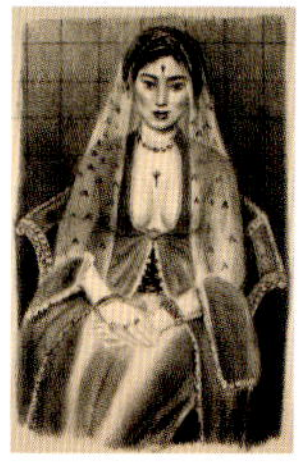

43. The Persian

1929. Crayon lithograph with scraping
Image: 17 5/8 x 11 7/16 in. (44.8 x 29 cm)
Sheet: 24 13/16 x 17 1/2 in. (63 x 44.5 cm)
Pierre and Tana Matisse Foundation (1245 - 101015)
Duthuit 507

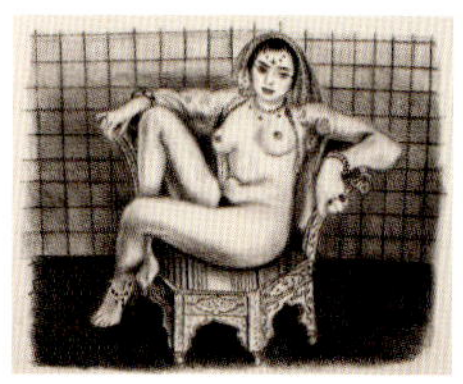

44. Young Hindu

1929. Crayon lithograph with scraping
Image: 11 1/4 x 14 1/8 in. (28.5 x 35.8 cm)
Sheet: 15 1/2 x 19 1/2 in. (39.5 x 49.5 cm)
Pierre and Tana Matisse Foundation (1006)
Duthuit 508

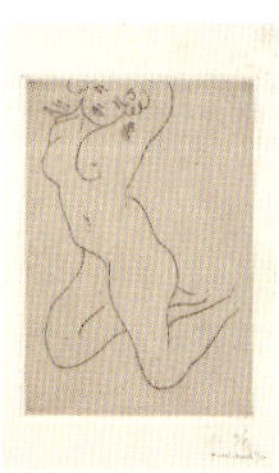

45. Kneeling Nude

1930. Etching
Image: 7 1/16 x 5 1/16 in. (18 x 12.9 cm)
Sheet: 14 15/16 x 11 1/4 in. (38 x 28.5 cm)
Pierre and Tana Matisse Foundation (1642 - 106025)
Duthuit 221
(p. 62)

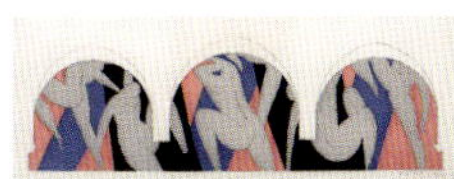

46. The Dance

1935. Color etching and aquatint
Image: 9 5/16 x 29 1/8 in. (23.6 x 74 cm)
Sheet: 11 11/16 x 31 3/4 in. (29.7 x 80.7 cm)
Pierre and Tana Matisse Foundation (1705-107037)
Duthuit 247

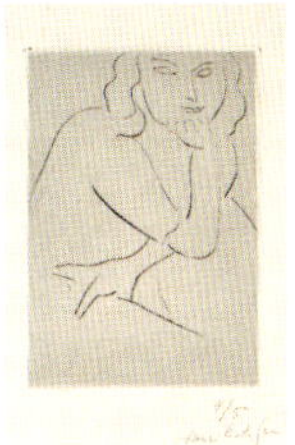

47. Young Woman with Transparent Eyes

1937. Drypoint
Image: 6 1/8 x 4 5/16 in. (15.5 x 11 cm)
Sheet: 17 3/4 x 12 3/8 in. (45 x 31.5 cm)
Pierre and Tana Matisse Foundation (1682 - 106068)
Duthuit 251

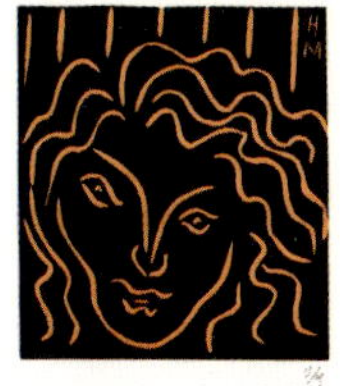

48. Head of a Woman, Mascaron

1938. Color linoleum cut
Image: 7 9/16 x 6 13/16 in. (19.2 x 17.3 cm)
Sheet: 15 3/4 x 11 13/16 in. (40 x 30 cm)
Pierre and Tana Matisse Foundation (1460 - 107016)
Duthuit 702

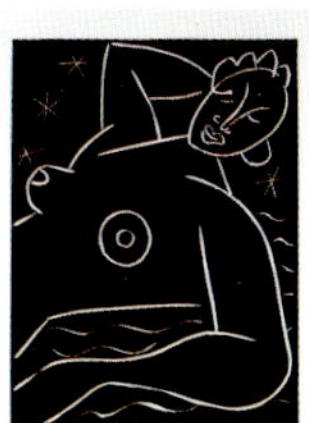

49. The Frigate

1938. Linoleum cut
Image: 12 3/8 x 9 7/16 in. (31.4 x 23.9 cm)
Sheet: 23 5/8 x 15 3/4 in. (60 x 40 cm)
Pierre and Tana Matisse Foundation (1461 - 107018)
Duthuit 703
(p. 63)

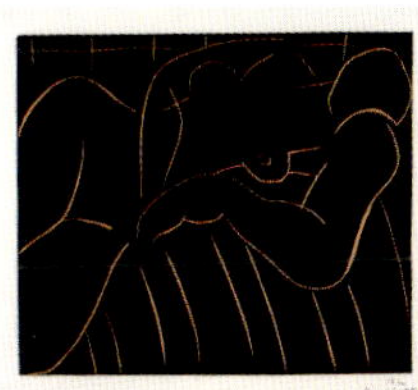

50. The Siesta

1938. Color linoleum cut
Image: 10 3/16 x 12 in. (25.8 x 30.5 cm)
Sheet: 15 15/16 x 18 1/8 in. (40.5 x 46 cm)
Pierre and Tana Matisse Foundation (1469 - 107031)
Duthuit 706

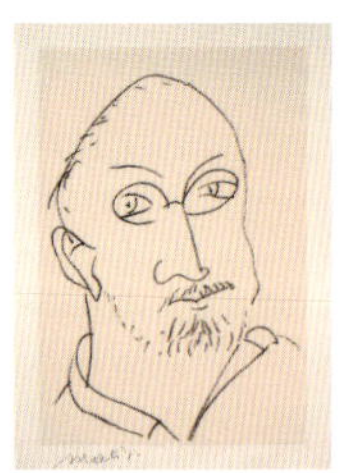

51. Large Mask
1944. Crayon transfer lithograph
Image: 13 7/8 x 9 13/16 in. (35.2 x 25 cm)
Sheet: 21 1/16 x 14 15/16 in. (53.5 x 38 cm)
Pierre and Tana Matisse Foundation (1369 - 103051)
Duthuit 562

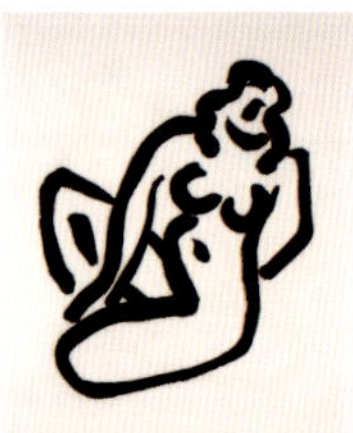

52. Crouching Nude I
1947. Lift-ground aquatint
Image: 13 11/16 x 10 7/8 in. (34.8 x 27.6 cm)
Sheet: 22 1/16 x 14 15/16 in. (56 x 38 cm)
Pierre and Tana Matisse Foundation (1451 - 104047)
Duthuit 781
(back cover)

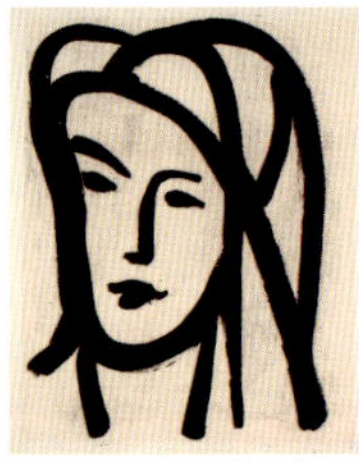

53. Bedouin with Large Veil
1947. Lift-ground aquatint
Image: 12 1/2 x 9 7/8 in. (31.7 x 25.1 cm)
Sheet: 19 7/8 x 14 15/16 in. (50.5 x 38 cm)
Pierre and Tana Matisse Foundation (1420 - 104015)
Duthuit 775

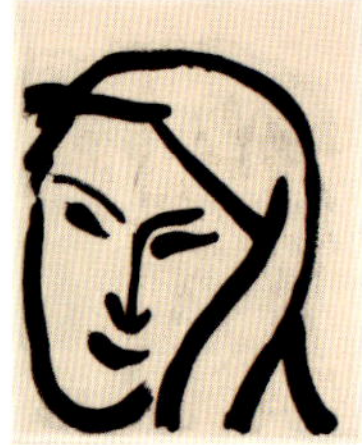

54. Bedouin with Untied Veil
1947. Lift-ground aquatint
Image: 12 1/2 x 9 7/8 in. (31.7 x 25.1 cm)
Sheet: 19 7/8 x 14 15/16 in. (50.5 x 38 cm)
Pierre and Tana Matisse Foundation (1419 - 104014)
Duthuit 779

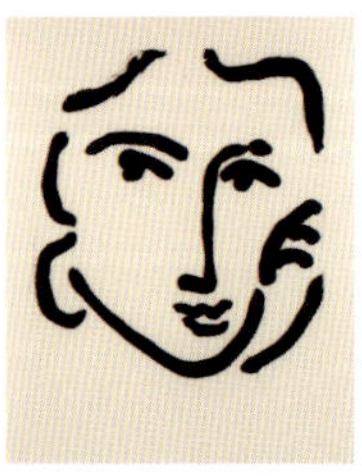

55. Nadia with a Serious Expression
1948. Lift-ground aquatint
Image: 13 9/16 x 10 15/16 in. (34.5 x 27.8 cm)
Sheet: 22 1/4 x 14 3/4 in. (56.5 x 37.5 cm)
Pierre and Tana Matisse Foundation (1411 - 104005)
Duthuit 793
(p. 70)

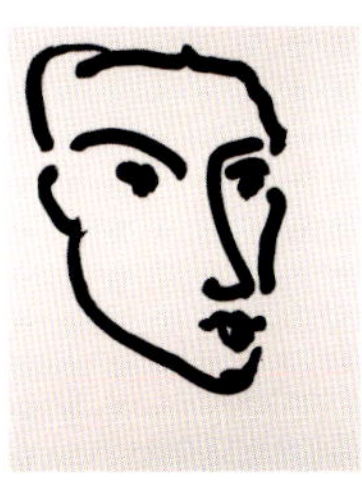

56. Nadia, Face in Three-quarter Profile

1948. Lift-ground aquatint
Image: 17 1/8 x 13 11/16 in. (43.5 x 34.8 cm)
Sheet: 26 x 19 11/16 in. (66 x 50 cm)
Pierre and Tana Matisse Foundation (1442 - 104038)
Duthuit 795

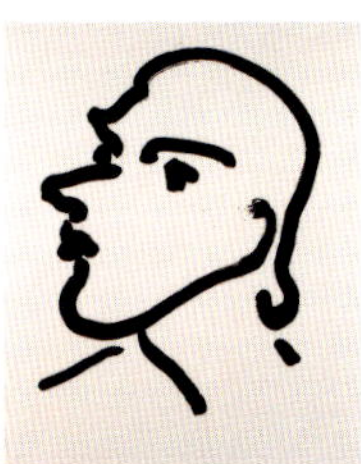

57. Nadia in Profile

1948. Lift-ground aquatint
Image: 17 1/8 x 13 11/16 in. (43.5 x 34.8 cm)
Sheet: 26 x 19 11/16 in. (66 x 50 cm)
Pierre and Tana Matisse Foundation (1438 - 104034)
Duthuit 804
(p. 33)

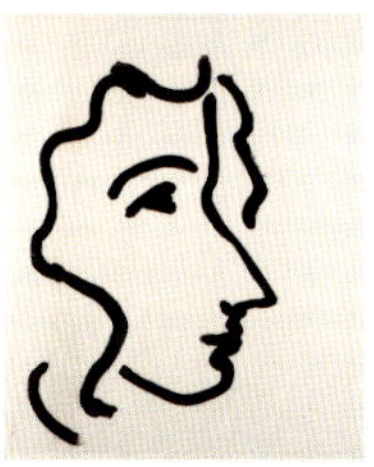

58. Nadia in Sharp Profile

1948. Lift-ground aquatint
Image: 16 15/16 x 13 3/4 in. (43 x 34.9 cm)
Sheet: 26 x 19 11/16 in. (66 x 50 cm)
Pierre and Tana Matisse Foundation (1430 - 104026)
Duthuit 810
(Frontispiece)

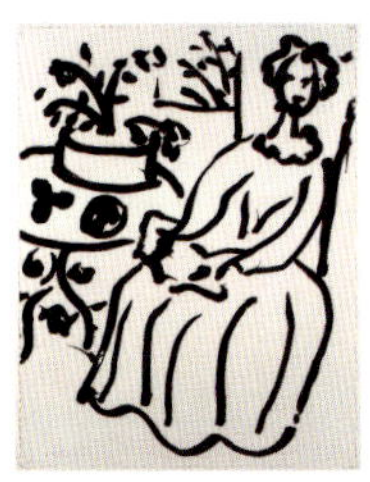

59. Marie-José in a Yellow Dress

1950. Lift-ground aquatint (black lines)
Image: 21 1/8 x 16 7/16 in. (53.6 x 41.7 cm)
Sheet: 29 15/16 x 22 1/4 in. (76 x 56.5 cm)
Pierre and Tana Matisse Foundation (2406)
Duthuit 817

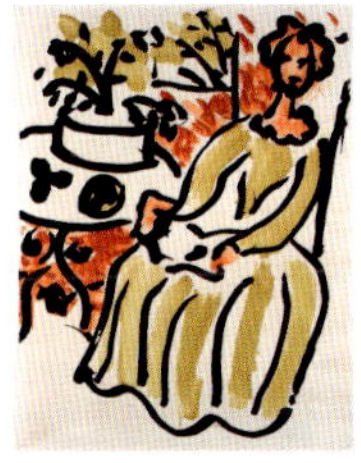

60. Marie-José in a Yellow Dress (I)

1950. Color lift-ground aquatint (black with two colors)
Image: 21 1/8 x 16 7/16 in. (53.6 x 41.7 cm)
Sheet: 29 15/16 x 22 1/4 in. (76 x 56.5 cm)
Pierre and Tana Matisse Foundation (1452 - 104049)
Duthuit 817

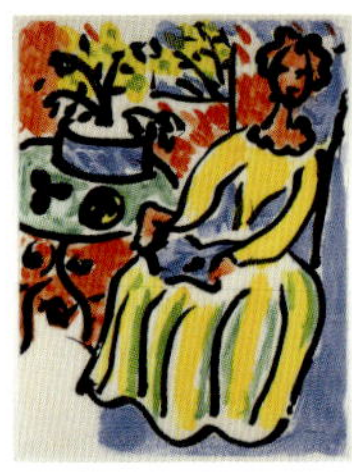

61. Marie-José in a Yellow Dress (III)

1950. Color lift-ground aquatint (black with four colors)
Image: 21 1/8 x 16 7/16 in. (53.6 x 41.7 cm)
Sheet: 29 15/16 x 22 1/4 in. (76 x 56.5 cm)
Pierre and Tana Matisse Foundation (1454 - 104051)
Duthuit 817
(p. 68)

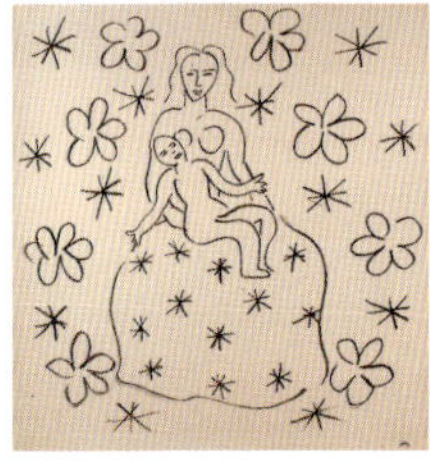

62. Large Virgin

1950–51. Crayon transfer lithograph
Image: 19 5/16 x 19 1/8 in. (49 x 48.5 cm)
Sheet: 25 3/8 x 22 1/16 in. (64.5 x 56 cm)
Pierre and Tana Matisse Foundation (1335 - 103004)
Duthuit 648

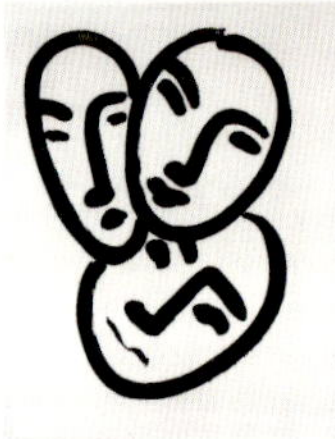

63. Three Heads. To Friendship (Apollinaire)

1951–52. Lift-ground aquatint
Image: 13 9/16 x 11 in. (34.5 x 28 cm)
Sheet: 20 7/8 x 15 9/16 in. (53 x 39.5 cm)
Pierre and Tana Matisse Foundation (1408 - 104002)
Duthuit 829
(p. 69)

Selected Bibliography

Barr, Alfred H., Jr. *Matisse: His Art and His Public.* New York: The Museum of Modern Art, 1951.

Breeskin, Adelyn B. "Swans by Matisse." *American Magazine of Art,* no. 28 (October 1935): 622–29.

Castleman, Riva. *Matisse Prints from The Museum of Modern Art.* New York and Fort Worth: The Fort Worth Art Museum and The Museum of Modern Art, 1986.

Duthuit, Claude. *Henri Matisse. Catalogue raisonné des ouvrages illustré,* in collaboration with Françoise Garnaud. With an introduction by Jean Guichard-Meili. Paris: l'Imprimerie Union à Paris, 1988.

Duthuit, Marguerite, and Claude Duthuit. *Henri Matisse. Catalogue raisonné de l'oeuvre grave.* In collaboration with Françoise Garnaud and with a preface by Jean Guichard-Meili. Paris: l'Imprimerie Union à Paris, 1983.

Elderfield, John. *Masterworks from The Museum of Modern Art.* New York: The Museum of Modern Art, 1996.

———. *Henri Matisse: A Retrospective.* New York: The Museum of Modern Art, 1992.

———. *The Drawings of Henri Matisse.* New York: The Museum of Modern Art in association with the Arts Council of Great Britain and Thames and Hudson, 1984.

Fisher, Jay McKean. "Sculpture Is Drawing Is Sculpture." *Henri Matisse: Painter as Sculptor.* New Haven: Yale University Press, 2007.

Flam, Jack D. *Matisse on Art.* Berkeley: University of California Press, 1995.

Girard, Xavier, and Sandor Kuthy. *Henri Matisse, 1869–1954; Skulpturen und Druckgraphik—Sculptures et gravures.* Bern: Kunstmuseum Bern und Autoren, 1990.

Hahnloser-Ingold, Margrit. "Matisse graveur." *Henri Matisse, gravures et lithographies.* Fribourg: Musée d'Art et d'Histoire, 1982.

———. "Notes sure l'oeuvre graphique de Henri Matisse," *Henri Matisse, gravures et lithographies 1900–1929.* Pully: Maison Pullierane, 1970.

Hahnloser, Margrit. *Matisse: The Graphic Work.* New York: Rizzoli, 1988.

Lambert, Susan. *Matisse Lithographs.* New York: Universe Books, 1982.

Lieberman, William S. "Illustrations by Henri Matisse." *Magazine of Art,* no. 44 (December 1951): 308–14.

———. *Etchings by Matisse.* New York: The Museum of Modern Art, 1955.

———. *Matisse: 50 Years of His Graphic Art.* New York: George Braziller, 1956.

Neff, John Hallmark. "Henri Matisse: Notes on His Early Prints." *Matisse Prints from the Museum of Modern Art.* New York and Fort Worth: The Fort Worth Art Museum and The Museum of Modern Art, 1986

O'Brian, John. *Ruthless Hedonism: The American Reception of Matisse.* Chicago: University of Chicago Press, 1999.

Russell, John. *Matisse: Father and Son.* New York: Harry N. Abrams, 1999.

Spurling, Hilary. *Matisse the Master: A Life of Henri Matisse—The Conquest of Colour, 1909–1954.* New York: Knopf, 2005.

———. *The Unknown Matisse: A Life of Henri Matisse—The Early Years, 1869–1908.* New York: Knopf, 1998.

Woimant, Françoise, and Jean Guichard-Meili. *Matisse: l'oeuvre gravé.* Paris: Bibliothèque Nationale, 1970.

Woimant, Françoise. *Henri Matisse: Donation Jean Matisse.* In collaboration with Marie-Cécile Miessner and with an introduction by Jean Guichard-Meili. Paris: Bibliothèque Nationale, 1981.

INDEX

Page references in italics refer to illustrations. All works are by Henri Matisse unless otherwise indicated.

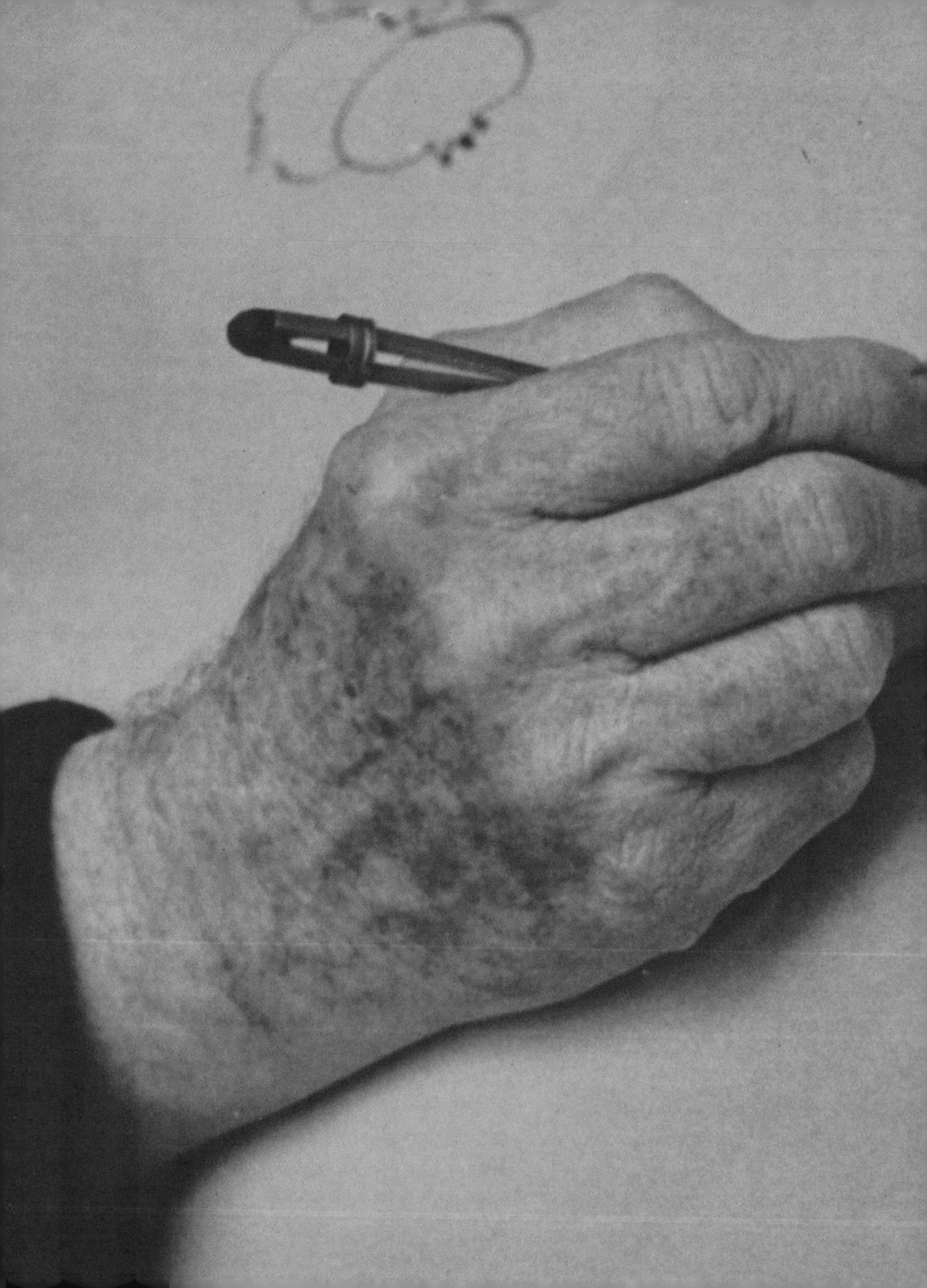